Bletchley Park Family - 1940 thr
Update 2017

Robert George Budd 1898-1969.
BP Security Photo.

Bletchley Park Family - 1940 through until 1950.
Update 2017.

Bletchley Park Family.
1940 - 1950
Up Dated 2017.
(Bletchley Park Fact)

By Neville J. Budd

Bletchley Park Family - 1940 through until 1950.
Update 2017.

Number 2 Cottage where we lived from 1940 until 1950. Photograph by Jean Budd.

Bletchley Park Family - 1940 through until 1950.
Update 2017.

© 2014 by Neville J. Budd. All rights reserved.

No part of this book may be reproduced, stored in a retrieval system, or transmitted by any means without the written permission of the author.

Because of the dynamic nature of the Internet, any web addresses or links contained in this book may have changed since publication and may no longer be valid. The views expressed in this work are solely those of the author and do not necessarily reflect the views of the publisher, and the publisher hereby disclaims any responsibility for them.

Neville J. Budd asserts the right to be identified as the author of this work in accordance with the Copyright Design and Patents Act 1988.

This book is sold subject to the condition it shall not, by way of trade or otherwise, be lent, resold, hired out, or otherwise circulated in any form without the consent of the author.

Bletchley Park Family - 1940 through until 1950.
Update 2017.

Dedicated to our family.
Robert George & Emma Rebecca Budd.
Robert George Edwin Budd.
Jean Mavis Budd.
Faye Patricia Budd.
Neville John Budd.

And the Golden Geese who NEVER cackled.

Bletchley Park Family - 1940 through until 1950.
Update 2017.

Front cover: Number 2 Cottage where we lived from 1940 until 1949. By Jean Budd.

Other photographs taken by our family, friends or Code Breakers.

Cover Design: Neville J. Budd

Edited by: Jean and Faye Budd.

In Collaboration with Jean & Faye Budd thank you for your help in making this book complete and also making my life full of happiness and love.

Acknowledgements:
Wikipedia.
Bletchley Archaeological & Historical Society.
(For bringing BP to the Notice of Influential People)
English Heritage.
Jean and Faye Budd.
Author Barrie Hyde. Photographs of D of Camb and Nev near Lake.

Bletchley Park Family - 1940 through until 1950.
Update 2017.

Other publications by the Author.

Fictional.

Murder Will Out, Book & Kindle.
Triptych of Stories, Book & Kindle.
A Very Able Seaman, Book & Kindle.
The King, Our Ships at Sea.
Love Letters from the Attic 1838. Kindle.
Short Stories of a Wannabe Writer.
Tail of the Fox.

Children's.

Island of Secrets 1, (Children's Books) Kindle.
Island of Secrets 2, Kindle.
Island of Secrets 3, Kindle.
Island of Secrets 4. Kindle.

Author Neville J. Anderson-Budd print books and Kindle.

Bletchley Park Family - 1940 through until 1950.
Update 2017.

Bletchley Park Family - 1940 through until 1950.
Update 2017.

Mr Robert George Budd

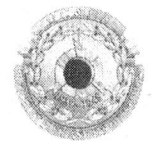

FO Civilian

For service in support of the work of Bletchley Park during World War Two.
We Also Served.

BLETCHLEYPARK
Home of the Codebreakers

Mrs Emma Rebecca Budd

FO Civilian

For service in support of the work of Bletchley Park during World War Two.
We Also Served.

BLETCHLEYPARK
Home of the Codebreakers

Bletchley Park Family - 1940 through until 1950.
Update 2017.

Mr Robert George Edwin Budd

FO Civilian

For service in support of the work of Bletchley Park during World War Two.
We Also Served

BLETCHLEYPARK

Master Neville John Budd

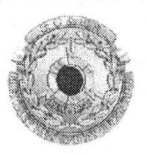

For service in support of the work of Bletchley Park during World War Two.
We Also Served

BLETCHLEYPARK

Youngest person to be admitted onto the 'Bletchley Park Roll of Honour'

Bletchley Park Family - 1940 through until 1950.
Update 2017.

Miss Jean Budd

Faye Patricia Budd

For service in support of the work of Bletchley Park during World War Two.
We Also Served.

BLETCHLEYPARK

Bletchley Park Family - 1940 through until 1950.
Update 2017.

These are the 2 types of badges issued to people who worked or were in Bletchley Park during WWII.
The big Gold badge is given to people who are still alive and worked in BP on Code Breaking work.
The bottom Red and Blue ones are given to people who lived in BP during WWII, both my Sisters and I are allowed to wear this one.

Bletchley Park Family - 1940 through until 1950.
Update 2017.

The Hidden Truth.

During WWII between 10,000 and 12,000 people worked in Bletchley Park, (Known as 'Station X' the 'X' stood for 10) the work these people carried out was extremely top secret, in fact Winston Churchill, who was a frequent visitor, often said "Bletchley Park was his and England's best kept secret" and the people who worked in the Park, "Were the Geese who never cackled." this secrecy extended to the very top of the Government and Military and lasted for at least 40 years which was 'THE HIDDEN TRUTH'.

The important work, which was being carried out by so many people at Bletchley Park, who did so much for our country but remained quiet about their achievements for so many years after because they were still covered by The Official Secrets Act, the trust and camaraderie was such an important part in the making of history in this world.

During this time the work carried out in Bletchley Park was the interception and breaking of the German codes, the best known being the 'Enigma Code' which had been in use for many years and the Germans considered unbreakable, the BOMBE machine designed and built by Alan Turing's team was used to break this code.

The LORENZ cipher was used by the top military echelons in the Nazi Military, this was the machine used by Hitler and the first ever-electronic Computer Colossus, was built there and used to break this code.

Bletchley Park Family - 1940 through until 1950.
Update 2017.

The ENIGMA cipher was originally designed to secure banking information. The German Military saw the potential in using the ENIGMA Machine and by the mid 1930's they saw its main use in its enciphering to be unbreakable, this they believed throughout the Second World War.

The odds against any success in the breaking of the code were set at 159,000,000,000,000,000,000 to 1. The 3 Polish crypto analysts Jerzy Różycki, Marian Rejewski and Henryk Zygalski obtained copies of the ENIGMA Machine and watched for modifications, which were being made. In July 1939 the Polish crypto analysts became aware of their countries danger and passed their knowledge and details of the BOMBA machine they had built, and at a secret meeting in the Pyre Forest to the governments of both England and France, the work these brave Polish men did helped to save at least 6 months work for the English in breaking the code.

It was agreed by England and France England should run with this information the reason being if the Germans overran France they would know we had the information to start to break the ENIGMA Machine.

The reason for the Polish Crypto Analyst naming the contraption they had built the BOMBA, which helped them to READ the coded messages the reason they could read the codes was because of the help a Captain Schmit (He liked Wine, Women and song also Women and Money) gave to them, he was the Brother of the Officer in charge in Germany of the Code and settings for the Coding Machine's, he did offer them to England and France but these two countries not knowing what they were to be used for did not accept them, the French directed him to the Polish who snapped them up.

They had intercepted an ENIGMA Machine which was being sent to the German's in Poland and managed to open it and inspect it VERY closely and make drawings and took photographs of the workings.

Realising what it would need to read the Coded Messages they set about making their small machine, the three of them had been in a group of about 150 other scientist and the Polish Government set out a test to find the most brightest Scientist they could, these three men were the only three left at the end of the test.

As they were contemplating what to call this device they were all sitting eating a beautiful Polish Ice Cream called a …………..

BOMBA.

So it was named after an ice cream.

When it was handed over to Alan Turing the name was kept but changed to BOMBE.

Bletchley Park Family - 1940 through until 1950.
Update 2017.

This is what the Polish Bomba Looked like.

Bletchley Park Family - 1940 through until 1950.
Update 2017.

The men who worked on the constructions were Dillwyn Knox, Alan Turing who invented the 'Bombe' an electro-mechanical machine with code wheels which reduced the time required to break the ever changing Enigma keys, he also wrote a treatise on a possible computing machine, and Tommy Flowers who was the Post Office Engineer in charge and his team of Electronic Engineers built Colossus. Many more people were involved in this work Bill Tutte and Gorden Welchman being a couple of the brilliant mathematicians along with a team of young ladies working in Number 3 Cottage who Dilly called the 'Harem' and the ladies were known as 'Dilly's Fillies'.

The first ever programmable electronic computer (Colossus) was 'Brain Stormed' by Alan Turing, (Who worked in Number 3 Cottage) Max Newman and Tommy Flowers who are now credited as the Fathers of the modern computer, also based on Alan Turing's ideas the world of computing and the Internet originated. Colossus was used to break the German Lorenz (Tunny) the encrypted German teleprinter traffic was known as "Fish" The Lorenz was used for High-Level German Military communications the machine had 12 wheels which contained 501 pins. There are quite a few different kinds of the ENIGMA machine used by the German Intelligence Service (Abwehr) the German Luftwaffe and Kriegsmarine the code used by the Abwehr was broken by Dilly Knox and his 'Harem' in 1941.

England and most of all the World owes the people who worked in Bletchley Park so much gratitude for the work they performed and in shortening WWII by at least 2 years saving millions of lives, no matter if they were the Code Breakers or the cleaning lady, they ALL had to sign the Official Secrets Act

Bletchley Park Family - 1940 through until 1950.
Update 2017.

which meant they could not talk about the important work which was carried out during WWII.

There is an incident of a married couple who visited Bletchley Park when it was opened up as a Museum, they were on a Guided Tour and the Guide said something and the wife blurted out "That is not correct" to which her husband said for her to be quiet as he was the Tour Guide and knew what he was saying, she responded by telling her husband that she had worked on that type of machine at Bletchley Park during WWII and she knew what the Tour Guide had said was wrong, the husband rather complexed at this and questioned about her working in BP which she said she had, the husband looked at her and told her then that he had also worked at BP during WWII, they had kept the secret from each other all of their married lives, this happened in the mid 1990's.

It was this self-denial which left many of them our unsung hero's during one of the most horrendous periods in history. So many of them could not get home to see their families, Many being ostracised by their families and others for not being in uniform and fighting, many were given the traditional 'White Feather' branding them as cowards as they could not tell ANYONE what they were doing, and sadly many of them lost loved ones but still carried on with this very important work at all hours and through their own sorrow, for that we thank them ALL and most important through all the years it has been……………………………………….

Bletchley Park Family - 1940 through until 1950.
Update 2017.

THE HIDDEN TRUTH.
NOW REVEALED.

Neville J. Budd.

Bletchley Park Family - 1940 through until 1950.
Update 2017.

The idea to write about our family and the time we spent living in Bletchley Park during WWII came about when Jean and I worked at the Bletchley Park Trust Shop with Roger Bristow, to make sure people know what happened there and to help save the Park which was due to be demolished, mind you we only attended for a short time as I was due to return to South Africa, another reason being our Sister Faye in Australia said she would be making a Wall Hanging about the Park, Faye at the time being a Lecturer in Quilting, she asked us for some idea's and I said I would write something………….big mouth that I am as I have never written anything but Project Procedures.

Faye asked me to write something about the Wall Hanging as we had been known and called 'The Children of the Park', it was the first time I had ever had to write anything about our lives and came up with the following, and called it:-

"Children of Bletchley Park"
1940 - 1950.

REMEMBER,
REMEMBER,
REMEMBER.

How do you remember important things which happened over 50 years ago, when at the time you were a child who only wanted to do childish things and did not understand what was going on around you, decisions which would change the whole future of this world.

Bletchley Park Family - 1940 through until 1950.
Update 2017.

People would say "Do you remember when ………." or "Do you remember so and so……." you would say "Oh! Yes I remember…….." but really it is only after these people have gone into more detail you do start to remember more and more of things which happened. So it was with myself when my Sister's and Brother asked me to put down in writing some of our memories of our lives as the "Children of Bletchley Park"

When all of this happened our family, that is the ones still about as sadly Mum and Dad had died, we were invited to the Park when it was to be opened by the Duke of Kent, the Wall Hanging was presented to him, eventually the Hanging was hung in the entrance of the Mansion for about 20 years with many people remarking about it and some ladies brought friends of their sewing groups to look at it, within the last 2 years it has been removed and now hangs in the Trust Meeting Room.

"CHILDREN OF THE PARK"

1940 to 1950.

Remember:

Remember:

Remember:

How do you remember things which happened over 70 years ago, when at the time you were children who only wanted to do childish things and did not understand what was going on all

Bletchley Park Family - 1940 through until 1950.
Update 2017.

around you, decisions which would change the whole future of this world.

People would say "Do you remember when ………" or "Do you remember so and so?" you may say "Oh! Yes I do remember………" but really it is only after these people have gone into more detail that you actually do remember more and more of things which did occur. So it was with myself when my sisters asked me to put down in writing some of our memories of our lives as the "Children of the Park"

Remember: Having the whole Park as a play ground, to climb the tallest trees and collect Duck Eggs from the Lake, oblivious to the important work which was being carried out by so many people.

Remember: Being told to keep quiet because the girls were working next door, we could never understand why, it got to the stage we were always tiptoeing around the house and whenever the telephone rang we were afraid that someone would hear us.

Remember: Being given Passes so we could go back and forth to our school in Church Green Road. Very often we would lose the passes, well sometimes we just mislaid them at home and in the end decided not to issue them to us any more, The Guards on Duty eventually got to know us, but it was big trouble if there was a new Guard on duty and he had not been informed about the "Children of the Park" we would have to walk all the way round to the Front Gate and not knowing our way home from there our Mum would have to come and collect three children with tears streaming down their faces.

Bletchley Park Family - 1940 through until 1950.
Update 2017.

After a while it became quite something to have armed soldier's watching over us until we were collected.

Remember: The day Mum went down to the Butcher near the Saracens Head in Buckingham Road to collect her ration of meat, it was lucky that Dad always kept a lot of chicken's, as Mum being a true Cockney would always take some fresh eggs or a chicken to trade for something more.

The day she went to the Butcher and returning back at the Main Gate and the soldier asking her for her pass:-

"Morning Ma'am can I see your Pass please?"

Mum searching frantically through her handbag.

"I am so sorry I seem to have left it at home, anyway you know who I am, Mrs. Budd I live here" Sorry Mum we children also tried that one, it doesn't work.

"I am very sorry Ma'am but no Pass means No Entry, this is a very High Security Area"

"But you know me"

"Maybe so Ma'am but No Pass means no entry, do you want to phone your husband?"

(I think the Guard felt sorry for us Children and was getting back at Mum and Dad for telling us off when we forgot our Passes)

Bletchley Park Family - 1940 through until 1950.
Update 2017.

Mum went to the Guard House and called Dad who came to the Main Gate.

"Yes! That is my wife and here is her pass"

Funny thing is we never got told off again after that..

Remember: The Hidden Garden near the Lake, where stories were told of Pixies and Fairies, Kings and Queens were held and of course only the most Very Important People were invited.

Remember: \building the big snow castles on the lawn opposite the Mansion and waylaying the people with snowballs as they were on their way and return from the canteen.

Remember: Your birthday party, with some of the girls from your class at Bletchley Road School, all gathered 0n the big lawn at the lake near the Magnolia Trees. (This could only happen when WWII had ended, it was only then we could invite our friends to our house).

Remember: The Disney faces and characters Bobby drew for the Christmas Dance in the Wilton Hall, with a big Father Christmas at the back of the stage behind the band. (They all seemed to disappear after the dance).

Remember: The New Year Dance when the Caretaker nearly fell through the ceiling so everyone knew the balloons were about to be let loose. The Caretaker was there to ensure Bobby did not fall, consequently Bobby had to rescue the Caretaker, mind you I think a lot of the people who were dancing heard

Bletchley Park Family - 1940 through until 1950.
Update 2017.

and learned a lot of very NEW words which Bobby called the Caretaker, bringing his whole family in disrepute.

Remember: The Christmas and New Year parties which were held at Number 2 Cottage, the front door was never closed to people who had to work over the holidays - they were always welcome. It was usually a knock on the front door and just wander in, getting a glass of beer from the 4 barrels dad always set up in the Hallway, then just drink and relax, singing along to some of the records of the time, or with Mum or Bobby playing the piano.

Remember: The big Christmas cracker Mum and Dad would make which use to hang across the corner of the living room, it was all of 7 to 8 feet long, Jean and Faye would pull it apart with the Crackers making a loud noise, and all the presents would fall down on coloured ribbons so we would know which ones were ours.

Remember: The drone of the aircraft flying overhead when we were in bed at night, the sound of their engines just went on and on and seemed to go up and down it was such a distinctive sound.

Remember: The sound of the bombs which dropped in the Park, just three of them out of about six, one just behind the Mansion and moving Hut 4 and the Sentry Box at the Back Gate, the next one landed just North of the Stable Yard but did not explode and was made safe the following day by the Bomb Disposal Squad.

Bletchley Park Family - 1940 through until 1950.
Update 2017.

It was always thought these bombs were dropped by the pilot to lighten his load so he could make it back to Germany, having probably lost his way and just dumped his bomb load.

Remember: The Search Lights south of us and the vapour trails from the planes overhead, at the time they looked so mysterious and beautiful but then we never knew what was happening up there.

Remember: The VE and VJ Services held in front of the Mansion, with all the flags flying and people dancing, hugging and kissing it was just like a big party.

AND.

Remember: We didn't have to keep quiet any more.

Bletchley Park Family - 1940 through until 1950.
Update 2017.

Bletchley Park Family.
(Fact)
By Neville J. Budd.

1940 to 1950.

How do you remember the most important things which happened in this world over 70 years ago, as like all other children of the period, all you ever wanted to do was childish things, play, climb trees, and stay out as late as you could, and of course you never did understand what was going on around you, decisions and actions which would change the whole future of the world.

Please remember, most of the things we do remember from our childhood are our memories and really cannot be verified as they are what I have said just memories and as you may know MEMORIES are the most treasured possession a child has and cannot be verified.

We are often asked if we ever met anyone important, to tell the truth we would never have known if they were important or not, to us the people who worked in the Park were just that 'Workers doing their everyday job', Dilly Knox, Alan Turing or Bill Tutte could have walked out of Number 3 going to lunch or to another place and we would not give them a second look because we did not know who they were.

Also one of Jean's memories of the time was when a tall dark haired man (who we assume was Alan Turing as it looked exactly like him so Jean and Faye say when they saw a picture

Bletchley Park Family - 1940 through until 1950.
Update 2017.

of him later) use to walk in our back door and say "Good night" and walk through the kitchen/dining room to one of the single bedrooms at the front of our house to visit who we assume was his mother as a lady of his mother's age was visiting us at the time.

Before we moved into Number 2 Cottage in 1940, another family lived there, this was the Hymer's family, Harry was a great friend of ours and when he was transferred to Naval Intelligence in London in 1939, Dad was offered the position he had at the Park.

Winnie Hymers.

We were close friends of the Budd family; Harry and Etty were Jean and Faye's God-parents.

Follows some of Winifred's memories which she wrote down about living in Bletchley Park:-

In 1938 my father changed his job.

This meant we had to move from our suburban house to a large rambling bungalow which had been converted from an old coach house and apple store.

It had three bedrooms on the ground floor and a big loft.

It fronted opened on to the stable yard and was part of the estate of a former Banker Sir Herbert Leon its name was 'Bletchley Park'.

Bletchley Park Family - 1940 through until 1950.
Update 2017.

We moved in at the beginning of the long summer school holiday and the only people living there were a gardener and his wife who lived in Number 1 Cottage, with a spectacularly vicious dog.

It was wonderful; we had the run of the estate, fields with sheep and cows and a nursery next door where we could buy all our fruit and vegetables, there were woods to explore and a small lake with a little boat on it; to us urban children it was a new world – MAGIC.

In September about thirty people came and stayed for a few weeks during the Munich Crisis and after they had gone all sorts of changes began to slowly take place; huts appeared on the lawns and some of the poplars were felled and replaced with aerial masts. Later a steel perimeter fence appeared and in due course we had guards and passes.

When the war started in September more and more people came with more huts being built.

THE RURAL IDYLL HAD GONE.

Billets were needed for all of the people and we always had two or three, my brother had left and I was banished to the loft where I had my bedroom and 'Den'

Our guests changed regularly, some of them were very eccentric and one of them insisted I learn the first ten lines of 'Paradise Lost' by heart, then another showed me how to solve

Bletchley Park Family - 1940 through until 1950.
Update 2017.

the 'Daily Telegraph Cryptic Crossword Puzzle' which I still do today.

They worked long and erratic hours and one of them learned I was learning French at school and would only talk to me in French. Some were less than discreet and would talk freely about what was happening in the War and many of these items were not announced on the Nine o'clock news until a few days later now this posed a problem for me in "Current Events" lessons at school, I could not always remember when I had heard some of the things, so I said nothing and was frequently reprimanded for my indifference to these important events.

I often heard the initials RDF and I asked one of our guests what they meant, he told me in some detail and said "You must not breathe a word of this to anyone" I instinctively knew I should not mention it.

At school I was often asked what was going on at the Park and I use to say "Only a lot of Civil Servants being evacuated from London"

In 1938 Harry Hymers and his boss Captain Ridley came to Bletchley. Winifred was 12 years old when they moved in and remembers the lake which had large carp which use to jump out of the water and get stranded on the large lily pads, also the sunken garden (our Hidden Garden) with its sundial.

One afternoon Winifred's father met her at the gate and took her into the Big House (Nowadays called the Mansion) this was always "off limits" we then went up the lovely wooden staircase to the first floor and I remember the three large William Morris

Bletchley Park Family - 1940 through until 1950.
Update 2017.

stained glass windows on the landing to the left of the stairs; they were 'Faith' 'Hope' and 'Charity'

Winifred was sent into a large room while her father waited outside and there was a long table covered with a grey army blanket with about five senior officers sitting at the table, in front of each one was a pad of papers and a pencil to one side of the pad. Their hats were in front of the pads and I noticed the peaks were all pointing in the same direction.

The officer in the middle looked very stern and started to question me:-

"Do you realise the very important and secret work is going on here?"

"Yes Sir"

"Do you realise it is vital that you do not discuss anything you may see or hear with anyone; not your friends, casual acquaintances; or anyone who may ask you questions"

"Yes Sir"

He then pushed a printed form across to me with a pen.

"You must sign this as a solemn promise you will keep your word"

I signed the form and no one else had spoken. I joined my father and as I closed the door I could hear laughter.

Bletchley Park Family - 1940 through until 1950.
Update 2017.

"Why are they laughing?" I asked.

He said "You are now the youngest person to sign 'The Official Secrets Act"

I was thirteen years old.

Winifred often went into the Mansion when no-one was in the Park and remembers the grand fireplaces the library and fluted pillars in the Ballroom.

The Hymers left Bletchley Park in 1940 when her father went to work at 54 Broadway. They were long standing friends of the Budd family who moved into No 2 Cottage. Her mother was Godmother to Jean of the Budd twin girls and Aunt Vera was Godmother to Faye; who stayed with the Hymers in 1938 when Neville was born.

Bletchley Park Family - 1940 through until 1950.
Update 2017.

Back to the Budd's.

Robert George Budd. Born 20/10/1898 Meean Meer India. Died 22/10/1969 Portsmouth.

Emma Rebecca Betchley. Born 08/06/1899 Bow, London. Died 14/02/1985 Luton.

Robert George Edwin Budd. Born 29/04/1925 Portsmouth. Died 08/04/2000 London.

Jean Mavis Budd. Born 20/04/1934.
Faye Patricia Budd. Born 20/04/1934.
Neville John Budd. Born 01/10/1938.

Dad joined the Royal Navy on 17th August 1915 at 16 years of age at HMS Ganges which was the Boy Training School at Shotley near Ipswich in Suffolk.

HMS Queen.

On the 6th of September 1916 he joined HMS Queen which is of the class Battleship built in 1902 and 15,000 tons with a complement of 750.

On the 14th of February 1917 he returned to HMS Victory 1 RN Barracks in Portsmouth.

Bletchley Park Family - 1940 through until 1950.
Update 2017.

HMS Raglan.

16th of March 1917 he was on board HMS Raglan which was a Monitor of 6,100 tons. The Raglan sailed for the Dardanelles in June 1917 and remained in the Mediterranean based at Imbros.

She was sunk on January 20th 1918 by the German Goeben off Imbros outside the Dardanelles. At this time Dad had been promoted to Able Seaman and was one of the few 127 of the Officers and men who survived; he was called to go with some of the other sailors who had managed to get overboard but decided to swim in the opposite direction which on his part was a VERY good decision, as about all of the other sailors were killed when the ship rolled. He returned to HMS Vernon on the 2nd February 1918 which was the Mine warfare school in Portsmouth.

HMS Glory 1

On 6th March 1918 she was used to land 130 Royal Marines at Murmansk to support the Bolsheviks as the brutal civil war erupted between the "Red" (Bolshevik), and "White" (anti-Bolshevik German and Finnish), factions.

She was then used as a depot ship until she was returned to the Soviet Navy in 1920.

On 6th October 1918 he was assigned to HMS Glory, which was a cruiser. She was seized by the Royal Navy during the Russian Revolution and commissioned as the Glory IV.

Bletchley Park Family - 1940 through until 1950.
Update 2017.

2nd of November 1919 he was once more at HMS Victory in Portsmouth, and on the 15th April 1920 through to 28th September 1922 was sent to HMS Barham and rated as a Leading Seaman.

HMS Barham.

HMS Barham was a Battleship of 37,450 tons and a compliment of 951 men.

1922 through to 26th of August 1925 he served at HMS Victory and Vernon.

HMS Columbine (Campbell)

In August 1925 he was sent to HMS Campbell, she was an Admiralty Leader Class Destroyer and was put in reserve in 1925 from being in service with the Atlantic Fleet.

In August 1927 he was sent back to HMS Victory at Portsmouth.

HMS Yarmouth

From September 3rd to 9th 1927 he work on HMS Yarmouth putting her into reserve, she was a Town-Class light Cruiser on the 15th he returned to HMS Victory Warfare School at Portsmouth.

Bletchley Park Family - 1940 through until 1950.
Update 2017.

HMS Dolphin.

In September 1927 he was sent to HMS Dolphin the Royal Navy shore establishment sited at Fort Blockhouse in Gosport.

HMS Dolphin was the home of the Royal Navy Submarine Service from 1904 to 1999 and location of the Royal Navy Submarine School.

He was there until September 1928 when he was sent back to HMS Victory again at Portsmouth and returned to HMS Vernon in November 1928.

HMS Revenge.

HMS Revenge was a Revenge class battleship in 1928 she was paid off for refit at Devonport Dockyard, Plymouth In January 1929 Dad joined HMS Revenge so he must have worked on the final part of her refit.

She was re-commissioned after the refit in March 1929 into the British Mediterranean fleet and in November 1931 he went back to HMS Vernon.

HMS Nelson

He had rose to the rank of Leading Seaman on the 1st September 1932 he was drafted to HMS Nelson which was one of two Nelson-Class battleships built for the Royal Navy between the two World Wars during his time at Nelson he rose to the rank of Petty Officer, he left her in January 1935 and

Bletchley Park Family - 1940 through until 1950.
Update 2017.

reported to HMS Excellent Naval Gunnery School at Portsmouth in August 1936 he was sent to his final ship HMS Danae and in January 1938 he went to the harbour to mothball her into reserve.

HMS Delhi.
The Delhi was a Danae class light cruiser.

In April he was sent to HMS Victory shore establishment until his discharge and on the 25th October 1938 he was discharged from the Royal Navy.

After our Father left the Royal Navy and we moved to Hayes in Middlesex in late 1938 we later found out Harry Hymers was my father's immediate boss and think it was he who arranged for our father to take over from him when he left his job at Bletchley Park.

We then moved to Newton Road in Far Bletchley, which is about a mile from Bletchley Park our mum and dad named the house JANFER which means 'Jean And Neville, Faye, Emma and Robert, our Father was employed at Bletchley Park between January and August 1939 and we moved into Bletchley Park in 1940.

I remember stories being told about an incident which happened while we lived at JANFER, this 'incident has been confirmed by the "Mighty Twins" my sisters and brother Bobby.

Bobby was told to look after me and it just happened we were upstairs in his bedroom at the back of the house.

Bletchley Park Family - 1940 through until 1950.
Update 2017.

I must admit I was a bit of a wanderer even at that age and Bobby was laying on the bed; possibly reading a comic or some such, and when he looked up to check on me all he saw were my legs disappearing over the window sill, at seeing this my ever diligent brother jumped off the bed and so I am told cleared ALL the stairs from top to bottom and ran out of the back door past a very scared Emma wondering why he was in such a hurry and hearing Bobby shouting something about Neville falling out of the window, they were expecting to see me splattered all over the pavement but even then I think someone was watching over me as what they found was Neville sitting in his pram laughing his head off, but the fact is now I hate heights.

In February 1940 our family moved into Bletchley Park, where we took up residence in Cottage No 2 in the Stable Yard this was after the Hymers family had moved out, Harry was sent back to work at the Broadway Buildings in London. (There was not enough room at BP so SIS and Diplomatic Service went back to London Feb 1942) Jean and Faye were 6, Neville was 2 and our older brother Bobby was 15 when we moved into the park.

As Harry Hymers was our father's direct boss this meant Dad was employed by SIS and the Diplomatic Service, but the work he carried out is still a mystery to our family, it is as if he was the 'Scarlet Pimpernel' in various books he is 'Head of Hut 2' in charge of Day to Day works, also we have found out he was in charge of all 155 Chauffeur's which daily collected the people working in the Park from their Billet's in the surrounding area, collecting and delivering the mail to the GPO in London, carrying messages to 54 Broadway in London, this

Bletchley Park Family - 1940 through until 1950.
Update 2017.

entailed them to drive approximately 35,000 miles a week, this was at the peak of when the highest number of people were working at BP.

He also headed the working party for day to day repairs and alterations at BP, Mansion Room Number 41, Main Administration Office of Mr. R Budd, In 1943 he was located in the main administration office and tasked with collating all outgoing private mail for posting in London, so as not to compromise the location of BP with its London FO Box Number.

The address for the Civilians working at the Park was:-

> Mr. Miss or whatever Title.
> BFPO Box 111.
> London.

For the WRNS it was different, the reason for this was all Naval personal working on shore Stations were stationed on what , in the Royal Navy are called Stone Frigates, this was so if asked where they were stationed they could honestly say they were at a Naval Base so the address for the WRNS: -

> WRN So and So,
> HMS Pembroke V,
> BFPO Box 111X.
> London.

Also Number 2 Cottage was designated as the home of the Quartermaster, Mr. Robert G. Budd so now you can understand why we call him the 'Scarlet Pimpernel', when we asked Mum

Bletchley Park Family - 1940 through until 1950.
Update 2017.

the usual question often asked by children, which was "What did Daddy do in the War" the answer was always the same "Don't ask me, he never told me a thing" and he NEVER EVER said a word about Bletchley Park during his life time, you know you should always trust your Mother to tell you the truth, well the truth of the matter was Mum also WORKED for the Foreign Office with Dad in Hut 2 and Brother Bobby became a Dispatch Rider and Driver also for the Foreign Office for Dad, none of them ever told us anything about what they did having all signed the Official Secrets Act.

From what we have managed to find out it seems he was employed by the Foreign Office (SIS) and the Diplomatic Service, from the description of what he was to do about all Private Mail and his 'Roll of Honour Certificate'

We are still looking for more and more information concerning what Dad did, some people think he was more involved within Bletchley Park and had a number of different jobs to cover what he really did, why would he and his family be living in BP when everyone else were put into Billets in and around Bletchley, why did he have a pistol hidden in the bedroom, why did he get calls at all hours of the night, these are some of the questions which we still think about. As the Quartermaster did his work involve Security, as we all know a 'Quartermaster' is a 'Regimental Officer in charge of securing Barracks'?

The other thing we have always thought about is why our family was allowed to live in the Park, it was either dad had a very important job or if there were German spies around they would think if children lived in the Park then it really could not

Bletchley Park Family - 1940 through until 1950.
Update 2017.

hold anything of much importance and they would never think about finding out what went on behind the high fence.

It is often said the people in Bletchley thought the Park was either a POW camp for German and Italian prisoners, or it was a Lunatic Asylum, which in a way was really closer to the mark when you think about how fine the line is between genius and insanity.

Think on that last thing when you understand that Alan Turing who suffered from hay fever use to ride about the Park wearing his Gas Mask, and lock his tin mug to the radiator in his office

Over the years you hear so many things about Bletchley Park you can understand some people being a bit dubious about what is said, the way things get exaggerated and told out of conjecture, one thing which I can use as an example is about Alan Turing hoisting his food up in the tower of Number 2 Cottage, it has also been said the tower is a 'folly' wrong again, the tower is the stairs for the upstairs in Number 2 Cottage, Alan Turing worked next door to us in Number 3 Cottage and yes he did hoist his food up at the window over the Back door, which in Number 3 Cottage is actually at the side of the house, the reason for this was he did not like going down stairs leaving his work and because the girls always were chattering away making too much noise.

Another thing which people joke about is Hitler, Goring, and the rest of his motley crew should contact Bletchley Park if they wanted to know what the messages said as BP were reading them in real time and before they had received them in their 'In Tray's'.

Bletchley Park Family - 1940 through until 1950.
Update 2017.

To have to rely on ones memory to recall significant activities after such a long period of time is so hard, things get blown all out of proportion or forgotten completely, so it is really advantageous a diary is kept of all of the important events which may occur during our lives.

How often people say to you "Do you remember when......." or "Do you remember so and so?" you always say "Oh! Yes I remember", but really it is only after these people have gone into more detail you do remember more and more, or is it some of their memories become entwined with yours, then you include them into the things you recollect and they all mould into one memory of the thing's which did happen. So it was with me, when my sisters asked me to put down in writing some of the memories of our lives as we became known as......

'The Children of Bletchley Park.'

During WW II Bobby was a dispatch rider and driver delivering messages to London and to the out laying areas such as Dorothy Perkin's in St. Albans. He was also driving the coaches picking people up from out-laying Billets and the Station and bringing them to Bletchley Park. Dear Father Oh! Father what were you thinking to have Bobby at 18 driving the coach which was picking up all of those unsuspecting WRNS and ATS girls of a similar age, and driving them to the Park. It was just as well he got married in 1945 to Eve Winifred Cobbett and had one daughter Evelyn in 1946, Eve and Bobby divorced and he married Hilda Fisher in 1952 they had five children: - Elaine,

Bletchley Park Family - 1940 through until 1950.
Update 2017.

David, Carol, Anthony and Jonathan. Whilst we were still living in the Park after the War, Bobby was able to join the Royal Navy as a Stoker/Mechanic and became one of the youngest to achieve the rank of Leading Hand long before his first four year stint and went on to become one of the youngest Petty Officers in his branch. I remember a couple of the ships he served on being HMS Warspite and HMS Striker, (Landing Ship, Tank (LST). Robert (Bobby) Died in April 2000.

Jean lives in Luton, England. She married John Walpole in 1955 they had three children Peter, Alan and Denise. Jean & John divorced and she married Peter Cheshire in 1988. During the time Jean was married to John Walpole they lived and worked in or around Luton. We both started with the Bletchley Park Trust with Roger Bristow in the shop in Queensway when it opened to help save the Park from being demolished as a housing estate.

Some notes about Peter Cheshire's Naval Service.

He joined the Royal Navy in February 1943 and Demobbed Sept 1946.

He was on board HMS Llangibby Castle with 557 Flotilland it was whilst he was on board this ship that he made the D-Day Landings on 6th June 1944 and landed the Canadian Force on 'Juno'

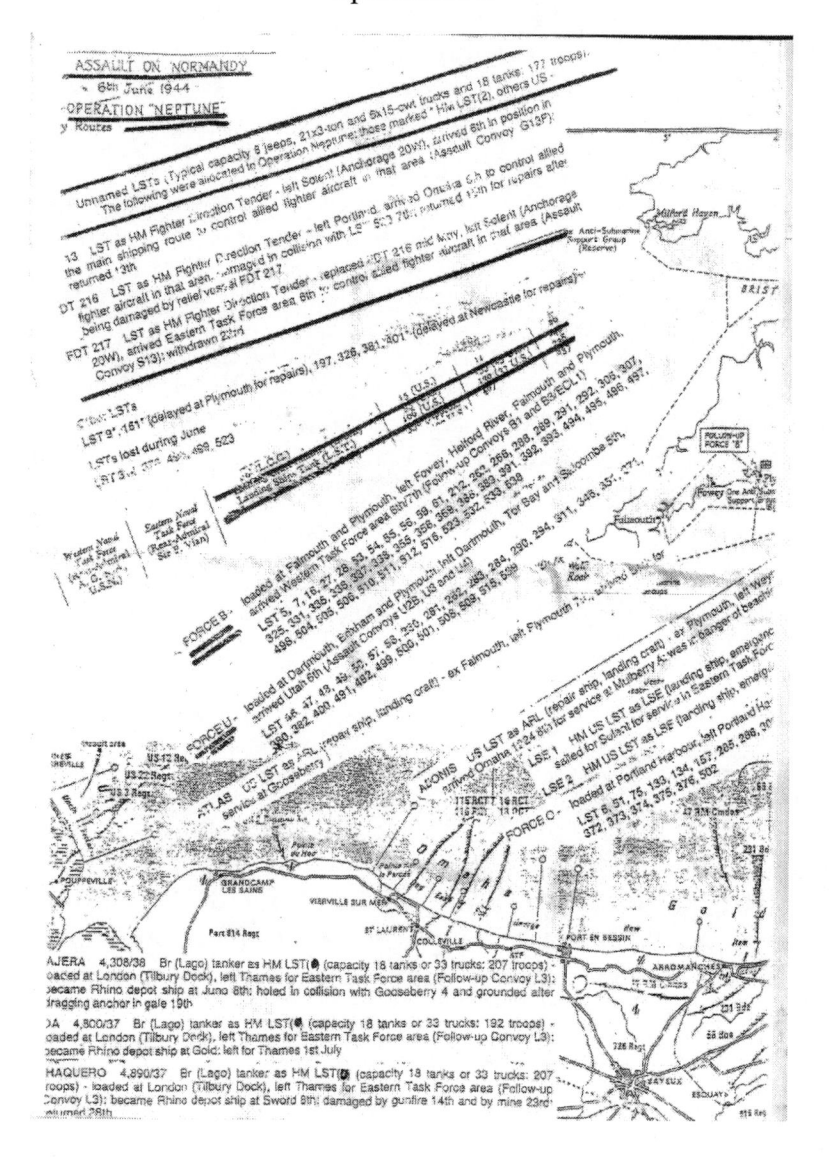

Bletchley Park Family - 1940 through until 1950.
Update 2017.

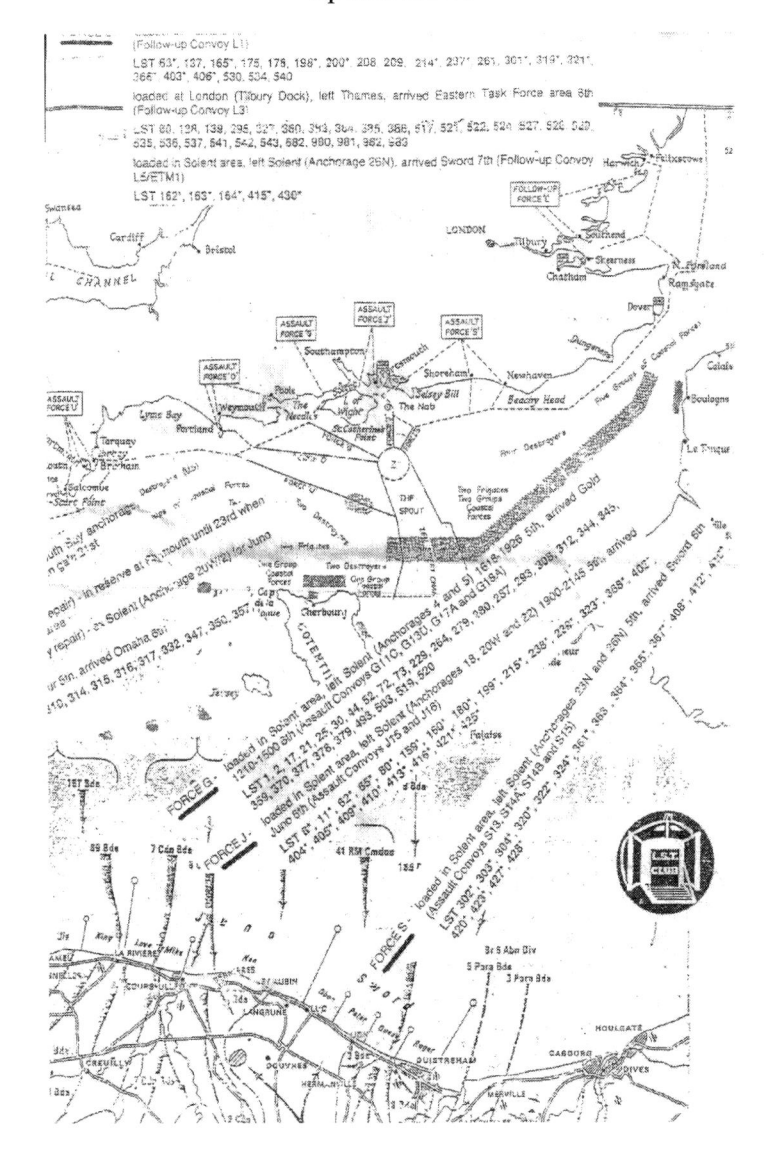

Bletchley Park Family - 1940 through until 1950.
Update 2017.

Bletchley Park Family - 1940 through until 1950.
Update 2017.

Jean has worked in Bletchley Park as a Steward for over 20 years. She has also been instrumental in giving 'Talks to various Groups such as the 'Women's Institutes' 'Women's Groups' and 'Historical Societies' about our lives in Bletchley Park, which is now the Museum for Code Breaking. I am sorry to say Jean is now getting tired of the travelling she has had to do and is cutting down on these activities and has asked (Asked is the polite way of putting it) me to continue them. Jean still does live a very active life as she goes dancing about twice a week and continues to do Quilting some of which can be seen in the entrance of the Mansion as she did help Faye with some of the sewing on the 'Wall Hanging' she still enjoys socialising.

One thing Jean remembers is Mum and Dad use to talk in 'Back Slang' if they didn't want anyone to listen to what they were saying.

- "**Back-slang** proper, sometimes employed by barrow-boys and hawkers, and indigenous to certain trades such as the greengrocer's and the butcher's, where it is spoken to ensure that the customer shall not understand what is being said ('Evig reh emos delo garcs dene'--Give her some old scrag end) consists simply of saying each word backwards, and when this is impossible saying the name of the letter instead of its sound, usually the first or the last letter, thus: 'Uoy nac bees reh screening O'Higgins (You can see her knickers showing).

- In the 1800s both these trades were popular among Cockneys it is no wonder that this masked dialect fed into Cockney rhyming slang.

Bletchley Park Family - 1940 through until 1950.
Update 2017.

Mum was a Cockney having been born in Bow.

Mum and Dad were chatting one evening and mum, using Back Slang asked Dad if he would like a biscuit or two with his tea, Jean popped up and asked if we could have some biscuits for tea also, I think she should have been employed with the Code Breakers as she had managed to pick out what Mum was saying, they were VERY careful what they talked about after that.

Another memory Jean has and shared with Faye and myself, was about us children playing 'Hide and Seek' around the back of the Mansion, next to Hut 4 which is now the restaurant, as we all ran out from the bushes Jean remembers seeing quite a number of men sunbathing IN THE NUDE, well Jean says we just ran as fast as we could as children do when they are surprised with something like that.

Faye Lives in Rosebud, Victoria, Australia with her husband Phillip Barnwell who she married in 1955 and has 2 daughters Lynn and Julie and from our conversations they lead a very energetic life, touring Australia, Scottish dancing and Faye give talks on embroidery, quilting etc. and who should be more knowledgeable as it was Faye who made the Wall Hanging which was on display in the Mansion for about 20 years and presented by our family to the Duke of Kent when he opened the Park in 1994 at Bletchley Park Museum. Faye and Phil have returned to England a few times and visited the Park whenever she can. Mum & Hilda did visit Faye in Australia a couple of times, Mum was in her 80's at the time.

Bletchley Park Family - 1940 through until 1950.
Update 2017.

Neville went to the Royal Hospital School (Formally Greenwich Hospital Boarding School now the Maritime Museum at Greenwich) in Holbrook just outside of Ipswich Suffolk in 1950 until 1955 where he became 'Head Boy' of St. Vincent and played Rugby for the school 1st XV for two seasons.

Neville had never before played Rugby, it had always been football which he never really enjoyed as he wasn't too good at getting the funny shaped ball to go where he wanted it to go, so when his House Master (Spud Tate) at St. Vincent decided they were going to put together a Rugby Team to play for the house and enter into the Inter-House Challenge, it wasn't a 'Will you play Rugby for the House?' it was more like 'You, You and You will be in the house Rugby Team' thank you 'Spud' as I did enjoy playing the game very much. Spud took all us 'Volunteers' out to the lawn outside the house and tried to teach us the fundamental rules of the "GAME", he must have done very well as for the first time in a very long time St.Vincent managed to win and become the Inter-house Champions and I was chosen to play for the school 1st XV and was awarded with my school colours twice.

I then served in the Royal Navy as a seaman and was put on P2 gun, a 4.7 as the Trainer, this is the man (man what a laugh I was 17 and a half) who trains the gun around from right to left onto the target, don't ask me why they did this to me as I had never been on a gun this size before in my life, anyway it eventually made me deaf in my left ear, so when they asked what branch I wanted to be in and they suggested gunnery I informed them I was not interested as they made too much noise and qualified as RADAR and Voice Radio Operator,

Bletchley Park Family - 1940 through until 1950.
Update 2017.

working in Hong Kong on Coast Watching Duties, Plotting and photographing Ships entering Communist Harbours, on leaving the RN I worked in Inspection starting in Non-Destructive Examination and became an Industrial Radiologist, and worked on various jobs around the UK, Europe, North Sea, Far East, Middle East and Persian Gulf, in 1979 I continued in inspection as a Quality Assurance/Quality Control Professional Engineer.

I lived in South Africa from 1990 through until 2013, with my wife Doreen Sarah Charnock who I married in 1959 and she died on the 27th November 2012, we had one son who was killed in a motorcycle accident in 1980, Neville returned to England in 2013 and now spends his time writing and being a Steward at Bletchley Park with Sister Jean.

Saturday 12th April 2014, I was at Bletchley Park as a Steward and as usual I had a great time I am happy to say and met so many people and had some good chats.

As I was going to the Bungalow (The Admin Office) to collect a magazine I came across one of the Tour Guides with her brood of tourist doing the tour. They now point out Number 2 as the place where the only family lived during the war and also tell them all our names, anyway one of the guides (Philomena) saw me and called to the other guide "Here comes Baby Budd" so the guide could introduce me, I did a quick curtsy and said Hi. Later when some people, from another group, came to where I was a Steward in the Book Shop and asking me some questions about the Park, I saw one of them looking hard at my ID badge, she then nudged her daughter and nodded to my badge, the daughter looked at it then at me and blurted out for all and sundry to hear "YOUR BABY BUDD" I didn't know

Bletchley Park Family - 1940 through until 1950.
Update 2017.

when and if to run, put my head between my legs and kiss my butt goodbye, think I went a bright red and promised myself I will kill Philomena when I see her next, seems the name will stick.

When you think back to the time when you were about five or six years old everything seems so different, always sunny, never ever a rainy day, unless of course you were due to go on a Nature Ramble, then of course it always rained and you had to stay in and have extra lessons in Math or English. But then when you got back home of course the sun always shone and for me that was great because I was a very lucky child during the war, I had the whole of Bletchley Park as a playground, let me explain about Bletchley Park.

Lord and Lady Leon had the Mansion built during the Victorian era, it is said and I cannot vouch for this but some people have said they feel a presence when they enter the Mansion and some have even said they have seen the ghost of Fanny standing at one of the upstairs bedroom windows, the interior was so beautiful, with stain-glass windows, wood panels, marble and oak floors, the main Hall as you enter had walls of wood and arches of granite supported by marble columns, the stairs were also made of marble which spiralled up to the main bedroom floor, but I think the most spectacular room's are at the back of the house on the ground floor, I am not sure what these room's were used for when Lord and Lady Leon occupied the Mansion, but I would think they were the most admired, I have since found out they were the Billiard and Ball Room's, I do not know of any person entering who would not have been lost for

Bletchley Park Family - 1940 through until 1950.
Update 2017.

words, these rooms were panelled throughout in wood, the walls were carved but this time with Romanesque columns with scroll work. The ceiling was covered with intricately carved panels decorated with scrolls, coat of arms and flora type patterns, looking toward the mansion on the right hand side where the road leads up to the clock arch and the old stable yard was the old dairy/ice-house which was like a small tower with a pointed roof, there are windows at the top of stained glass, on the other side of the house is another round tower with a bell shaped roof covered in copper, now green with verdigris in colour, this side of the house use to be covered ivy with flower beds and lawns which became the site for Hut 4.

The Wall Hanging which was hanging to the right of the entrance of the Mansion Hallway and was presented to the Duke of Kent for Bletchley Park Code Breaking Museum on behalf of our family.

If you look closely you can see the outlines of Mum hanging out the washing, Dad walking to work, Jean and Faye going to school at the back gate, Bobbie walking down by the lake being chased by the ducks and Nev on his bike so to speak!!!

There was an explanation of how it was made, the meaning of the Morse code which is threaded throughout the wall hanging, what the colours which surround the Hanging mean.

Follows in her words is an extract from some of and Faye's memories:-

Bletchley Park Family - 1940 through until 1950.
Update 2017.

We were born in the Royal Naval and Marine Hospital which use to be along Southsea front in Portsmouth; our Mother did not know she was expecting twins, which was lucky for Faye as she was the second one born after 15 minutes of labour after Jean was born.

Dad said to Mum it was fate; so she became named as Faye. We moved to Middlesex, and then to Newton Longville Road, Bletchley where we had our sixth birthday, the Postman had a bit of fun with us trying to remember which twin to give which card.

Our first memories of Bletchley Park was when Jean and I went to stay with Aunt Etty (Hymers) for a few days, one morning we went down for breakfast and she gave us half an egg each, she explained it was because we were twins.

From about this time Bletchley Park became our home.

Another memory Faye has is climbing up a small stair way behind Dad in the Mansion; the steps were very big to me at the time, it was here the ENIGMA Machine was kept "What a surprise". From this time we had a very happy home life and attended St. Mary's school in Church Green Road.

When we were at St. Mary's and in the play-ground on our birthday the other children use to sing "Hitler's twins, Hitler's twins" around the playground, this was because our birthday was on the same day as his – April the 20th.

Another memory was going into the pigeon loft and seeing some eggs which had just hatched, of course at the time we had

Bletchley Park Family - 1940 through until 1950.
Update 2017.

no idea what they were used for, but every day they would fly above the house.

We would go down three or four steps at the end of the courtyard, next to the bungalow into the Hut (Hut 2) at the bottom which in the early days was the Social Hut and remember "helping dad" bringing him the empty glasses to wash up, a bit later the Social Hut was moved to the other side of the Mansion, also in the same area was the Paper Kiosk the man in there would sit knitting socks in between selling papers. We never went to the new Social Hut until after the war as we were not allowed to go any further.

Number 2 Cottage never seemed empty; if someone was off duty we would have them in for a meal and Mum was a very good cook. We had two ATS girls living with us Anne MacDonald (later she married and became Mrs Anne Witherbed) and Madge Taylor. We always had lovely Christmas Parties, not a thing in the house until Christmas morning, we would wake up to a fairyland where every room would be decorated and anyone not on duty would pop in; what fun we children had.

We use to play all the old fashioned games, Blind Man's Bluff, Charades, Ludo as big as the dining room carpet with the dice the size of a brick, but my favourite was Colonel Puff and I remembered the whole rhyme and became a Colonel, I was so proud the children use to do it with water but the adults had beer in a pint glass and it was filled up every time you made a mistake, we use to think they made a lot of mistakes on purpose so they would have more to drink.

Bletchley Park Family - 1940 through until 1950.
Update 2017.

Another memory was at about this time Jean and I went with Anne and Madge to Scotland, Jean to Kirkcaldy with Anne and I went to Edinburgh with Madge it was a time when they were on leave.

I also remember the train was packed and everyone was being so kind and ready to help we were so tired we had to sleep across the solders knees that were also asleep.

When the war had ended things seemed to happen so fast, Jean and I would go with Mum to the Social Hut (During the War this was Hut 4) into a room where a man was playing billiards, he said for me to have a game, so that was when I learned to play billiards mind you I was only just tall enough to reach the table, I also learned to play shove ha'penny, in another room some girls were making sandwiches and I have never seen anyone cut up a cucumber so fast, they told me there was going to be a dance in the evening; I seem to remember Mum and Dad taking us in for a short time.

From then on it seemed we had the whole Park to ourselves, nobody in any of the houses in the Courtyard and even the pigeons had gone.

What has happened? Where is everyone? The Park was empty and even the guards had gone.

What a fun time we had so much to explore, what were all these huts for? And Dad took us rowing on the lake and we thought can we really go anywhere we want to on our own?

Bletchley Park Family - 1940 through until 1950.
Update 2017.

The day I found the Sunken Garden I knew I had found the place where the Fairies lived and Dad would ask "Where is Faye?" the answer was she's off with the Fairies; it wasn't until years later I realized the pun in it.

I came back to Bletchley Park in 2003, the Sunken Garden was all overgrown and nobody seemed to know anything about it; but I knew it was there. It is now in the process of being restored.

We lived in the Park for another five years and saw a lot of changes, first Mr and Mrs Holt moved into the bungalow with their two children Roger and Wendy, then the Saunders family with three children Diana, Janice and Graham moved in to Number 1 and after a while there was a lot more people about and this was when the GPO took over and used it as a training centre and a teachers training college, there was so much going on then and we had much more freedom.

Mr and Mrs Jenkins moved in to Number 3 cottage with their children David and Jane and I am still friends with Jane, we played table tennis in one of the huts (Hut 12) and had more adventures and freedom together and then the Saunders moved out and Mr and Mrs Arkell and their daughter Betty moved into No 1 Cottage.

We were getting older now and all going in different directions, Bobby our oldest brother was in the Royal Navy, Jean and I were still at Bletchley Road School and Neville was off to the boarding school Royal Hospital School at Ipswich, Suffolk, then all of a sudden we were all in the work force.

Bletchley Park Family - 1940 through until 1950.
Update 2017.

It was 1950 and now the time to leave the Park.

My life continued to be an adventure, I married Philip Barnwell in 1955 and we have two daughters Lynn and Julie and two grandchildren Sarah and Lauren we all have travelled to lots of interesting places and all now live in Victoria, Australia.

Mum and Dad became licensees of the Plough Inn at Simpson and Dad was working for the Diplomatic Wireless Service at Hanslope Park, we think this is when he knew Burgess, Maclean and Philby, and then he and Mum were off to Singapore for a couple of years.

A memory I do not have is why did we lived in the Park?

And what did my father do all those years?

Faye Barnwell.

Bletchley Park Family - 1940 through until 1950.
Update 2017.

During the time I have been a Volunteer Steward at Bletchley Park and meeting so many visitors I have been asked many questions, some are about our family and what was it like to live in the Park during WWII, or did we every meet Alan Turing, Dilly Knox or any of the other people working there, the answer of course is "We may have done, but at the time did not know what was happening or who they were".

Jean and I have met so many nice people and always spent time with them mostly they are very pleased to meet someone who was actually there and we both have had so many photographs taken with these great visitors.

Some of the Tour Guides do mention the 'Family' who lived at Number 2 Cottage in the Stable Yard and usually tell them that either Jean or myself are there as Volunteer Stewards and they may find us in the Mansion, 'B' Block or in 'C' Block, I did have one lady come into the Ballroom in the Mansion and looking around spied me and came rushing over pointing at me, at the time I was trying to think if we had ever met and what if anything we had in common, when she stood in front of me she said "Are you Neville" standing a little bit further away from her I nodded, she then took off for the door, I just looked around and quite a few of the other visitors were laughing and some were wagging their fingers at me asking "What have you been up to?" after about 10 minutes she returned with about 8 other people and pointing at me "This is Neville, he is the one the Guide told us about" when she pointed and said "This is

Bletchley Park Family - 1940 through until 1950.
Update 2017.

Neville" my knees started to buckle and then she finished and a lot of people around me started to laugh.

Another question is "Why is the machine Alan Turing and his team built called the 'Bombe' this I did explain earlier in the book.

Then it is why was the film called the 'Imitation Game' when the exhibition was open in the Mansion of the film I often called everyone's attention and asked them why it was given that title as most of them had seen the film, so many, well just about everyone just looked at me and shook their heads, so I then had to enlighten them:-

In 1950 Alan Turing wrote a paper called "Computing Machinery and Intelligence" while he was working at the University of Manchester.

He started by asking the question "I propose to consider the question, 'Can machines think'" from this he proposed a game of 4 people and Turing's new question is "Are there imaginable digital computers which would do well in the *Imitation Game'* he believed this question can actually be answered. In the remainder of the paper, he argued against all the major objections to the proposition that "machines can think".

Another question always asked is "Was Bletchley Park ever bombed?"

I have to be honest and tell them "Never as a target" but on a quiet night of the 20th November 1940 a single aircraft probably

Bletchley Park Family - 1940 through until 1950.
Update 2017.

destine to bomb Wolverton Carriage Works north of the Park dropped a stick of 6 bombs.

Number 1. Landed at the corner of Rickley Lane, just off Church Green Road, it landed in the front garden of a beautiful white thatched cottage and on exploding left a very large crater and a crack down the front of the cottage which sadly had to be demolished as it was too dangerous.

Number 2. Dropped near the Stables at Elmers School which at the time was used by WRNS as their Billet, nobody was hurt.

Number 3. Fell just SW of the Mansion and close to the Guards Sentry Box at the Back Gate, which you can still see the damage to this day, it was closer to Hut 4 and the explosion lifted the Hut off its footings and moved it about 2 feet, it was jacked back into place and the work did in the Hut did not stop.

Number 4. Landed to the North of the Stable Yard and NOT in the Yard as many people state, this bomb did not explode and was made safe the following day by the Bomb Disposal Corp.

Number's 5 & 6 landed in some fields to the North where Block 'F' was eventually built.

The question mostly asked is "How and why was Bletchley Park chosen to become the Code Breaking Centre during WWII?"

This one can be a little long:-

Bletchley Park Family - 1940 through until 1950.
Update 2017.

The House was first built about 1871 and a Samuel Seckham became the owner in 1877 who it is thought was the main builder.

Shortly after the Mansion was completed in 1883, Seckham sold the property to Herbert S. Leon.

Herbert Leon made extensive enlargements and alterations mainly based on some of the houses he and his wife visited thinking that they would look nice if they were added to their place, this is the reason for so many different types of architecture.

Herbert S. Leon died in 1926 and his wife died in 1937.

The Mansion and grounds were put on the market but did not sell, it was then placed in an auction and eventually sold to a Mr. Hurbert Faulkner for the princely sum of £7,500, he began to strip out all of the fixtures and fittings of the house before he was going to demolish it to start and built a house overlooking the lake for himself and on the rest of the estate he was going to build houses for sale.

It was in 1937 when Admiral Sir Hugh Sinclair who was a British Intelligence Officer between 1919 and 1921, he became the Director of British Naval Intelligence and set up the Secret Intelligence Service (SIS, known as MI6) before WWII.

On hearing about Bletchley Park being sold he organised 'Captain Ridley's Shooting Party to visit and assess the possibility of BP becoming a 'Wartime Intelligence Station'

Bletchley Park Family - 1940 through until 1950.
Update 2017.

On reporting back to Admiral Sinclair the Party informed him it was "Suitably situated in the countryside North of London, close to the A5 road which ran North from London, there was a main railway Station at Bletchley with links to Oxford and Cambridge, and also there was a Main Relay Sub Station at Fenny Stratford, so it was really ideal for an Intelligence Station to be situated there"

Admiral Sinclair approached Mr. Faulkner and and made an 'Offer' he couldn't refuse, this was for the Admiral to purchase the Park, he had already approached numerous Government Departments for money to buy BP but these had all been refused, so he offered Faulkner £7,500 (this would be of his own money) or he would have the Park under the Compulsory Purchase Act, also he offered that Faulkner would have the Contract to erect builds as required, Mr. Faulkner accepted his offer.

Throughout the war (1939-45) it accommodated various sections of GC&CS, including the Directorate.

Admiral Sinclair became very ill with cancer and died on the 4th November 1939 at the age of 66.

As far as can be ascertain the Park still belonged to him on his death.

So Bletchley Park became a very important part of English history.

Bletchley Park Family - 1940 through until 1950.
Update 2017.

Mum and Dads wedding 29th August 1923 at Saint Paul's

Church Southsea Hampshire.

Dads Mother Kate Anderson on the left of Dad

Bletchley Park Family - 1940 through until 1950.
Update 2017.

Dad died on the 22nd October 1969, Mum died on 14th February 1985.

Bletchley Park Family - 1940 through until 1950.
Update 2017.

REMEMBERING ROBERT AND EMMA BUDD
THEY LIVED AT NUMBER 2 COTTAGE 1940-50.
WITH CHILDREN BOBBIE, JEAN, FAYE, NEVILLE

Kenneth Foster

Marion Eaton
née Hendry

Lytton
/Sinclair

Robert G & Emma
Budd & Family

Geoffrey C
Catherin

Edith Ivy Horne
née Adams

Janet Bruce
née Alberta Miller

The Morse letter 'V' on the bottom of the brick is for 'Veteran'
The wall can be seen as you walk towards the Mansion passed 'A' & 'B' Blocks.

Bletchley Park Family - 1940 through until 1950.
Update 2017.

Grand Ma Betchley, we think that is Mum's brother on her knee.

Bletchley Park Family - 1940 through until 1950.
Update 2017.

Mum in the front row second from right when she was a Silver Service Waitress in Southsea at the age of 16 years

Bletchley Park Family - 1940 through until 1950.
Update 2017.

Dad on the right when he was in the Royal Navy.

Our father (on the left this time) played the clarinet & Saxophone he was in the Grenville Dance Band he was also taught Morse code.

Bletchley Park Family - 1940 through until 1950.
Update 2017.

Bletchley Rail Station.

Janfer 1940 Newton Road.

Bletchley Park Family - 1940 through until 1950.
Update 2017.

Faye, Nev & Jean with Mum Aug 1940.

Bletchley Park Family - 1940 through until 1950.
Update 2017.

Dad & Nev 1940, that's the pram I landed in when I fell out of the upstairs window. The dog was called Max.

Bletchley Park Family - 1940 through until 1950.
Update 2017.

Robert George & Emma Rebecca Budd at Hayling Island.

Jean, Neville and Faye with Marcia Thorpe in the Garden of No 2 Cottage Bletchley Park.

Bletchley Park Family - 1940 through until 1950.
Update 2017.

Jean, Mum, Dad and Faye, with Nev in front at Number 2 Cottage.

Dad holding Brother Bob's daughter Bab's at Number 2 in the background is Hut 11a.

Bletchley Park Family - 1940 through until 1950.
Update 2017.

Hut 2

Bletchley Park Family - 1940 through until 1950.
Update 2017.

HUT 2

Timber outer shell constructed by Aug 1939 under supervision of Capt Faulkner. Located just to the north of the front of the Mansion and east of Hut 1, just south of Huts 9 and 9A. Issued cups of tea, sandwiches and sold luncheon vouchers throughout the War and from Feb 25 1943 was also permitted to sell beer over lunch and tea times, in its official role as the "Recreation Hut". It may also have been referred to by BP staff (particularly Service men and women) as the NAAFI Hut. Hut 2 also housed the lending library run by Mrs Vivian until May 1942, when she left BP and moved to London with her husband and most other SIS staff based at BP. This freed up rooms in the Mansion, so the BP Recreational Club and the lending library were moved from Hut 2 to former dining rooms in the Mansion. From mid-1942 Hut 2 was used two evenings a week for Naval Section language classes (one evening for German, one for Italian). By June 1944 Hut 2 was being used as a Casualty Reception Station during "BP in danger" ARP exercises. Hut 2 was under the supervision of Mr Budd. It was finally demolished in 1946 to make way for a car park.

HUT 2A

Intended location for the Transport Office in July 1941 but in fact this moved to Room 2 of Hut 9, (located at a right angle to and just north of Hut 2), two months later. There is no other evidence for a Hut 2A, so it is possible that the intended 2A was incorporated into the adjacent Hut 9.

Extracts from 'History of Bletchley Park Huts and Blocks 1939 – 1945'.

Bletchley Park Family - 1940 through until 1950.
Update 2017.

Bletchley Park - January 1940

Bletchley Park - January 1940

Skating on the Lake.

Bletchley Park Family - 1940 through until 1950.
Update 2017.

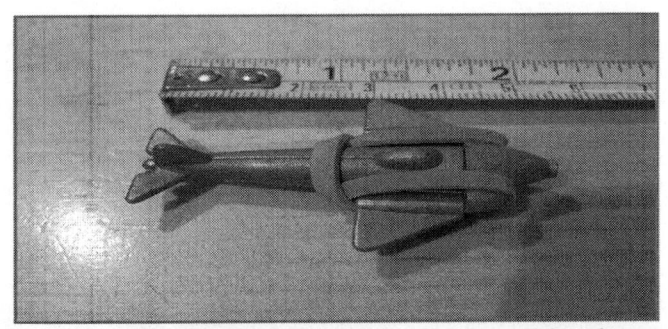

Photograph of the Cap Bomb we use to play with. Photograph taken by Mr. Kevin Coleman and reproduced here by kind permission of Mr & Mrs Mark and Min Cornelious who own the Holley/Cornelious Collection of Domestic Artefacts and Playthings 1930's – 1950's and was situated in Bletchley Park.

Replicas of Dinky Toy Cars from the Fredrick Rautenbach collection South Africa.

Bletchley Park Family - 1940 through until 1950.
Update 2017.

Jean, Faye and Neville at the steps leading down to the Croquet Lawn near the Lake (Sorry I do not remember the young boys name)

Bletchley Park Family - 1940 through until 1950.
Update 2017.

Some of Jean & Faye's friends from Bletchley Road School at their birthday party just after the war.
Back Row Pam Missenden (Smith) Joy Amos, Margery Griffith, Faye Budd
Front Row Neville Budd, Margaret? Jill Chew, Judy Blogg, Jean Budd

Bletchley Park Family - 1940 through until 1950.
Update 2017.

Dad in Singapore 1958/59.

Bletchley Park Mansion.

Bletchley Park Family - 1940 through until 1950.
Update 2017.

Block 'C', Dad was the Manager of this block from 1945 – 1950. All the furniture was collected for redistribution to London and other WD Premises including GC.HQ.

Mum and Dad in Hayling Island.

Bletchley Park Family - 1940 through until 1950.
Update 2017.

"The Children of Bletchley Park". (Jean, Bobby, Neville and Faye.) (Photograph taken near the Clock Arch leading to the Stable Yard at Bletchley Park).

Bletchley Park Family - 1940 through until 1950.
Update 2017.

Bletchley Park Post Office

The part of the mansion now housing the Toy Museum and Post Office was originally part of the Kitchen and Butler's pantry and bedroom complex. The Post Office outbuilding was built prior to 1990 and this room prior to 1925 for use as a scullery.

During World War Two it was used as a receiving room for Bletchley Park mail under the jurisdiction of the Quartermaster Mr Robert (Bob) Budd.
Mr Budd lived in Bletchley Park Cottage No 2 with wife Emma, twin daughters Jean and Faye, sons Robert (Bobby) and Neville until 1950.
Eldest son Bobby often took mail to the Dorothy Perkins store in St Alban's to avoid the suspicions of enemy agents.
Around 1947 the GPO created the little post office for people attending post war training courses at Bletchley Park.

Robert Budd
Quartermaster
Bletchley Park
1942 - 1950

Jean, Bobby,
Neville and
Faye in 1947

Bletchley Park Family - 1940 through until 1950.
Update 2017.

Signatures of people who worked at the Park on the back of the picture of the Mansion.

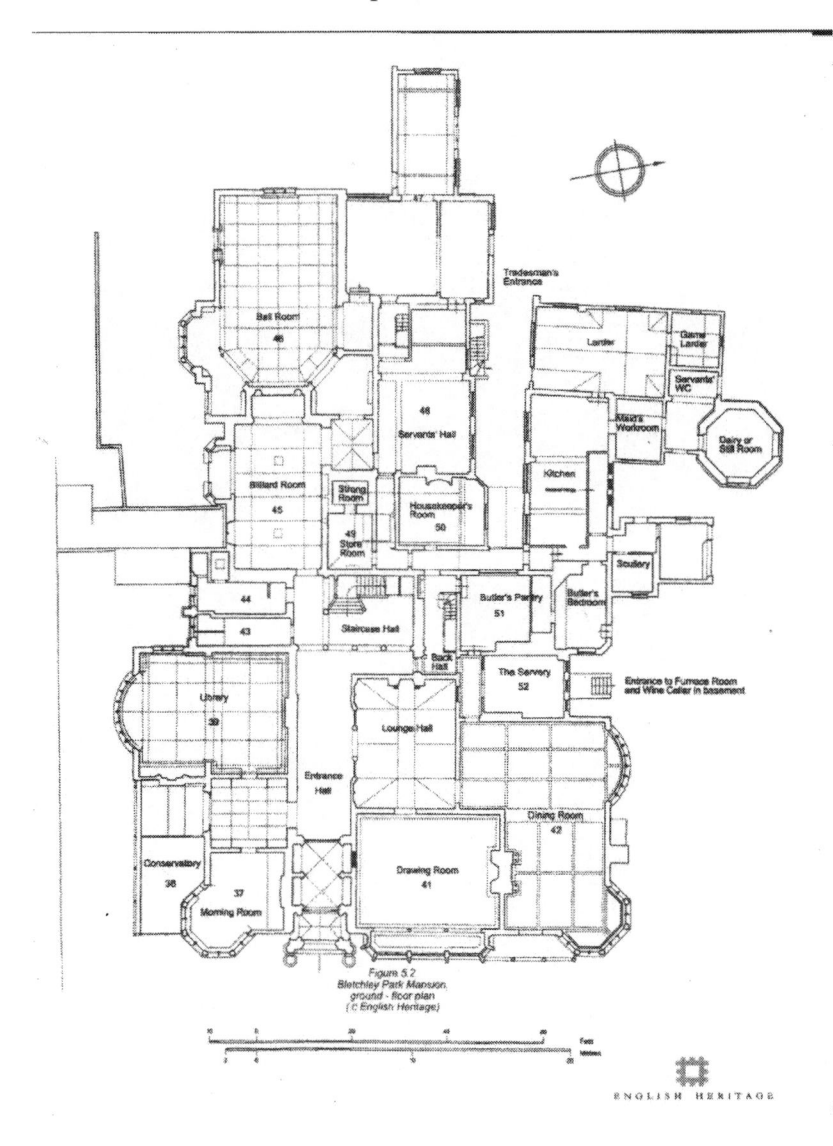

Bletchley Park Family - 1940 through until 1950.
Update 2017.

Figure 5.2
Bletchley Park Mansion,
ground - floor plan
(© English Heritage)

ENGLISH HERITAGE

Plan of the rooms on the ground floor of the Mansion.
Room 41 is where Dads Office was situated.

Bletchley Park Family - 1940 through until 1950.
Update 2017.

Figure 5.0-3
Bletchley Park mansion,
first - floor plan
(c English Heritage)

Plan of the rooms on the upper floor of the Mansion.

Bletchley Park Family - 1940 through until 1950.
Update 2017.

Lake and Small Island where the ducks use to nest.

The road we use to take to the Back Gate to go to School.

Bletchley Park Family - 1940 through until 1950.
Update 2017.

The Approach to our school St. Mary's in Church Green Road.

St. Mary's present day it is now two houses. An old section of the school can be seen on the left of the picture.

Bletchley Park Family - 1940 through until 1950.
Update 2017.

Our Hidden Garden as it is today; but it is due to be restored to its original beauty in the near future.

Brother Bobby's wedding at St Mary's Church, Church Green Road 1945.
Dad & Mum on the left. Neville in front of Dad & the two bridesmaids Jean on left and Faye on the right.

Bletchley Park Family - 1940 through until 1950.
Update 2017.

Jean, Hilda & Bobby & Mum. (Bobby looks really 'Chuffed' with himself)

Bobby, Hilda, Elaine & David at the Plough Inn, Simpson.

Bletchley Park Family - 1940 through until 1950.
Update 2017.

Faye & Phil Oct 1955.

Group picture of Jeans wedding. (Mum and Dad on the right)

Bletchley Park Family - 1940 through until 1950.
Update 2017.

Number 2 Cottage where we lived from 1940 through to 1950.

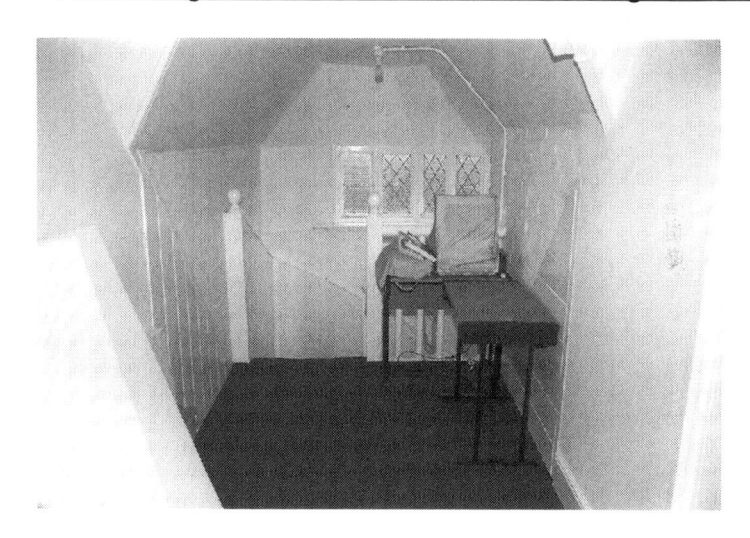

Stair Tower at No: 2 Cottage

Bletchley Park Family - 1940 through until 1950.
Update 2017.

The Plough Inn Simpson where we lived when we left Bletchley Park in 1950 -1958.

Bletchley Park Family - 1940 through until 1950.
Update 2017.

Nev's School, Royal Hospital School Holbrook, Ipswich.

Bletchley Park Family - 1940 through until 1950.
Update 2017.

R.H.S Inter-house Junior Rugby Champions St. Vincent 1953.
Hood, Parker, Neville (Captain) Baker, Clooney, Harding.
Letley, Hall, Lloyd Willock, Frost, Savage.
Robinson, Glen, Anderson.
(Neville Later got his school colours twice for the school 1st XV for 2 seasons.)

Bletchley Park Family - 1940 through until 1950.
Update 2017.

Nev third from the left top row, outside St. Vincent House 1954 Royal Hospital School, in uniform Head Boys of the House.

Bletchley Park Family - 1940 through until 1950.
Update 2017.

Faye, Jean, Bobby best man, Neville, Sally, Des Turney who gave Sally away, Hilda (Sally's Mum) Barbara (Sally's Sister) David (Bobbies Son) Theresa & Lynn (Barbara's Daughter's) Elaine Bobbie's Daughter. 25th July 1959. All Saints Leighton Buzzard.

Bletchley Park Family - 1940 through until 1950.
Update 2017.

Able Seaman Neville Budd HMS Ocean 1955.

Bletchley Park Family - 1940 through until 1950.
Update 2017.

HMS Birmingham November 1956 flying Battle Ensigns for Suez.
Nev served on board as Gun Trainer 4.7 P2 and Damage Control when at Cruising Stations.

Nev with Jane Jenkins bit of a Tomboy if I remember who use to live at Number 3 Cottage Bletchley Park. (Sister Faye in background on the far left.

Bletchley Park Family - 1940 through until 1950.
Update 2017.

At the dedication by the Duke of Kent and Professor Thewlis when the Duke opened Bletchley Park as a museum in honour of the Code Breakers who work on the ENIGMA Code during WWII.

Bletchley Park Family - 1940 through until 1950.
Update 2017.

THE BLETCHLEY PARK TRUST WISHES TO THANK

The Trust wishes to acknowledge how much we appreciate our visitors being with us today.

During the war the folk at Bletchley Park had a reputation of meeting whatever was asked of them, often with very little or no notice.

These exhibitions that you will be able to see from 1:15pm, today, have been gathered and installed within the last four weeks. This task has been undertaken by volunteers, supported by many local companies and individuals.

On behalf of The Chairman and Trustees we wish to thank those who have helped and supported us since the Trust was formed. Their assistance has been vital to the Trust in reaching its aims and objectives. This mutual friendship will ensure the ongoing success of the Bletchley Park story.

Bletchley Park Trust Aims and Objectives.

To secure for the nation the area known as Bletchley Park in recognition of the work of the Intelligence Forces carried out at the site between 1939-45, particularly in relation to the breaking of enemy codes.

To develop on site museums of cryptology and the history of computing as Bletchley Park was the home of the world's first electronic computer in the 1940s and is recognised as the birthplace of the computer industry.

To encourage any other museums development on the site, particularly of a high-tech nature.

To supervise and encourage commercial initiatives on site to assist the on-going funding of the museums complex as above, so long as these initiatives are compatible with the overall aims and objectives of the Trust.

WELCOME

to the

FORMAL OPENING

of the

BLETCHLEY PARK TRUST

EXIHBITIONS

and the

COLOSSUS RE-BUILD PROJECT

in the presence of

H.R.H. DUKE of KENT

18 JULY 1994

BLETCHLEY PARK TRUST

INVITATION
TO ATTEND THE

ROYAL OPENING
OF THE
BLETCHLEY PARK EXHIBITIONS
BY
H.R.H. DUKE of KENT
ON
MONDAY 18 JULY 1994
TICKET No. 0552

THIS TICKET IS NOT TRANSFERABLE
ENTRANCE GATES WILL BE CLOSED AT 10:30 am.

Bletchley Park Family - 1940 through until 1950.
Update 2017.

BLETCHLEYPARK

The Chairman,
Trustees and the Chief Executive Officer
of the Bletchley Park Trust
request the pleasure of the company of

Mr Neville Budd

at a reception in Bletchley Park to mark the completion
of the first phase of its restoration

in the presence of HRH The Duchess of Cambridge

on Wednesday 18 June 2014 1000 hrs to 1400 hrs

Pour memoire   Dress code: Lounge suit or ladies equivalent

Bletchley Park Family - 1940 through until 1950.
Update 2017.

Tuesday, June 24, 2014 www.leightonbuzzardonline.co.uk

NEWS

Codebreakers

Honoured to be a guest for royal visit from Duchess

BY STEVE SIMS
news@lbobserver.co.uk
01522 795512

A Leighton Buzzard man who lived at Bletchley Park for ten years during the 1940s was thrilled to be an invited guest for a royal visit from The Duchess of Cambridge.

Neville Budd, 75, of Hockliffe Street, looked on as the Duchess visited on Wednesday. It marked the completion of the £8 million restoration of Codebreaking Hut 6 and she also saw the vibrant new Block C Visitor Centre.

He said: "The new entrance to Bletchley Park is now Block C, which after the Second World War our father was the manager. He worked in Bletchley Park with the Foreign Office from 1940 until 1950."

Neville revealed that after the war he and his sisters had played in Block C on many occasions. He said: "We were very sad when we left the parks as we had lived there for ten years and remember it as our garden."

He added that both he and his brother and sisters had also been invited to Bletchley Park when the Duke of Kent opened it as a museum in 1995, with his sisters presented the wall hanging which is now on display in the mansion.

Of last week's royal occasion, Neville said: "The Duchess wore a blue and white dress with gold buttons and looked most elegant. I feel very honoured and proud to have been at the opening and feel this way because of the work carried on by everyone who worked there during the Second World War. They helped shorten the war by at least two years and kept the secret for so many years after, but we are so proud of our dad."

Both Neville and his sister Jean are volunteer stewards at Bletchley Park – where the Duchess' grandmother worked during the war.

The Duchess of Cambridge at Bletchley Park, and inset, Neville Budd

Bletchley Park Family - 1940 through until 1950.
Update 2017.

ROLL OF HONOUR
By Neville J. Budd

From 1939 through until 1950 our father worked in Bletchley Park. That is, during WWII, we, the family of Mum, Bobby, Jean/Faye and I moved into Number 2 Cottage in the Stable Yard. We were the only family to live in the Park during this time. Next door at Number 3 Cottage were Alan Turing, Dilly Knox, and about a couple of dozen WRNS (Women's Royal Naval Service), who were busy breaking the German ENIGMA and LORENZ codes. To break the ENIGMA code was 159 million, million, million to 1 and that was with 6 wheels. The LORENZ had 12 wheels so was much harder to break. Also working was Tommy Flowers a very talented Government Post Office (GPO) Engineer who with his team built the first electronic programmable computer called Colossus. Number 34 Cottage was known as the Harem because of the number of women who worked there and the girls were known as Dilly's Fillies. Mum always told us to be quiet as the 'girls' were working next door. Dad was employed by the Foreign Office and held the position of, wait for it, Security, Transport, and Post and also acted as the Administration Manager. These positions were of utmost security when you think of the work being carried out there. Security of the whole Park which meant that nobody will say anything about the work they did, not even to the people they worked with. Transport was used to collect and return the people to their lodgings, and there were between 10,000 and 12,000 people working during the war and 133 drivers to collect them to work 3 X 8 hour shifts every day. They covered a total of between 30,000 and 35,000 a week. This included taking and collecting messages down to 54 Broadway, Naval Intelligence and Dorothy Perkins in St. Albans which was a drop off point. The post was delivered to the Post Office in London, for the WRNS. It was BFPO Box 111X, HMS Pembroke V., and for the other workers, BFPO Box 111. The reason for it being a Stone Frigate for the WRNS was so members of their family would understand they were stationed at a Shore Station. They couldn't really have letters addressed to "Bletchley Park Code Breaking Service." It was great when I managed to find out what Dad did in the Park during WWII and find out we were ALL mentioned on the "Roll of Honour."

all photos courtesy Neville Budd
Neville Budd at Bletchley Park

Bletchley's Roll of Honor certificate

#2 cottage at Bletchley Park where the Budd family resided

CORRY STATION GETS A PIECE OF I.B. ANTENNA

A piece of the last Navy CDAA is now on display at the Command Display onboard Corry Station, Pensacola, Florida. A low-band antenna base and the low-band insulator are pictured below along with a model of a Wullenweber antenna array

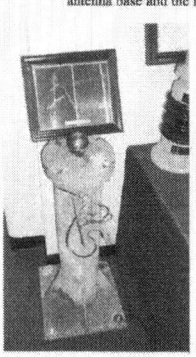

Bletchley Park Family - 1940 through until 1950.
Update 2017.

D of Camb at the opening of the new Entrance in 'C' Block.
(Picture by Author Barrie Hyde)

Bletchley Park Family - 1940 through until 1950.
Update 2017.

18th June 2014 at the opening of the New 'C' Block Entrance
by HRH Duchess of Cambridge.
(Picture by Author Barrie Hyde)

Bletchley Park Family - 1940 through until 1950.
Update 2017.

Neville with 'The Mighty Twins" in South Africa on Durban's North Beach. October 2010.

Bletchley Park Family - 1940 through until 1950.
Update 2017.

First time back at BP after returning from South Africa after 24 years with the 'Mighty Twins' 2013.

Bletchley Park Family - 1940 through until 1950.
Update 2017.

The Bletchley Park Wall Hanging

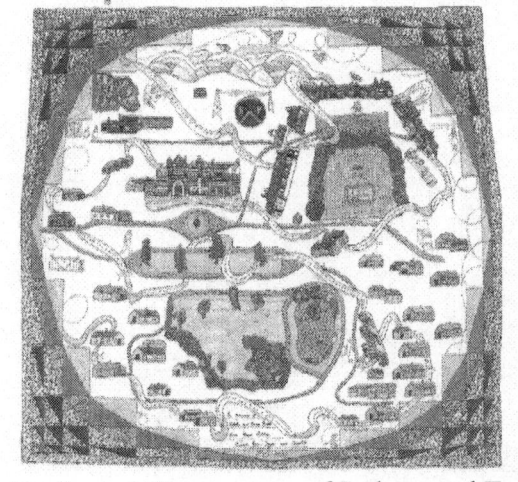

The Mansion

Cottages 1, 2 & 3

Dedicated "In memory of Robert and Emma Budd from their children Robert, Jean, Fay and Neville."

Faye Barnwell (Nèe Faye Patricia Budd) made the Wall Hanging and these are the notes descriptive which hang next to it in the Mansion.

Making the Wall Hanging brought back many happy memories for me.

Taking some News Papers to people from the Paper Kiosk where a man used to sit knitting socks and I collected empty glasses for Dad from the tables in Hut 2, going to the pigeon loft to see the eggs which were just about to hatch. The ATS girls who stayed with us, the church service held outside the Mansion after the War. Then suddenly there was nobody left in

Bletchley Park Family - 1940 through until 1950.
Update 2017.

the Park and what a wonderful playground we had. We could go anywhere we wanted.

Then it was off to work, riding my bicycle to work at W.O. Peak's making Rodex Coats, where I learned my trade as a seamstress. This has been a great help to me over the years with my craft work. I went to live in Australia with my husband Philip Barnwell and two daughters Lynn and Julie in 1965 where I have won many first, second and third prizes at Craft shows, including the Royal Melbourne Show.

This is my second pictorial, the first being of the 'State of Victoria' which has been in many exhibitions. The Bletchley Park wall hanging took one year to make, being machine pieced and hand appliqués in buttonhole stitch. Hand quilted into the wall hanging is our family. Quilted, because nobody seemed to know children were there. Dad is walking to work, Mum hanging the washing out, Bobby running from the geese – they always chased us. Jean and Faye going to school and Neville riding his bike. Also Radio Pylons, a Rose for Peace, a Maze where the tennis courts now stand, an ENIGMA Machine, front and back station gates and wire on top of the fencing around the Park. The Grey area, top left hand corner is the Spinney outside the Back Gate. The Music notes read 'There is no place like home'

Bletchley Park Family - 1940 through until 1950.
Update 2017.

The border is Symbolic in three ways.

1. Representing the perimeter of the Park.
2. Radio Waves.
3. The sky at the beginning of the war, when it gets darker and darker and finally at the end of the war there is a blue sky again.

The Morse code reads from the bottom left hand side:-

1. GC and CS (Government Code and Cypher School)
2. Sick Bay.
3. Intelligence Service.
4. Army.
5. Navy.
6. Air force.
7. Job up.
8. Enigma.
9. Good morning Mr. Budd.
10. Ultra Secret.
11. Royal Signals.
12. Paper Kiosk.
13. Colossus.
14. Bombe's.
15. Station X.
16. The Bungalow.
17. Universal Machine.
18. Peace.

I belong to the Mornington Peninsula Patch workers Inc.. in the state of Melbourne.

Bletchley Park Family - 1940 through until 1950.
Update 2017.

We are not sure if Evelyn wrote these, because she did write a lot of poetry.
Eve wife of Bobbie Budd Married 1948.
<u>Tree's</u>

I think that I shall never see
A site as curious as BP.
This place called up at War's behest
And peopled with the strangely dressed.
Yet what they did they cannot say
Nor ever till judgement Day.

For six long years we have been there,
Subject to local scorn and stare.
We came by transport and by train,
The dull ------brilliantly sane.
What were we for, where will we be,
When God at last reduns B.P.

The Airforce types who never fly,
Soldiers who neither do nor die,
Landlubber sailors, beards' complete,
Long-haired Civilians – slim, effete!
Why they were there they never knew
And when they told it wasn't true.

If I should die think this of me,
I served my country at B.P.
And should my son ask "What did you
In the Atomic World War Two"-
God only knows and He won't tell –

Bletchley Park Family - 1940 through until 1950.
Update 2017.

For after all B.P. is Hell.

MUST WE LEAVE THE OLD HOME, MOTHER?

Must we leave the Park, Director
Where we've lived for many a year
Must we at this time effect a
Transfer far away from here?
Round the place rumour's sweeping
Gaining strength from day to day,
Edward, Sir, why are you weeping
Oh! Must we leave the old home say?
CHORUS. Must we leave the Park Sir Edward
Tell me won't you, must we roam
Must we wander to the Eastward
Far away from the old home?

Must we leave the Park, Director
And forsake it once for all
Shall we have in the new sector
Both Beer Hut and Assembly Hall?
Are we really so repugnant
That you can't bear us to stay?
Must we be declared redundant
Oh! Must we leave, Director, say?

Bletchley Park Family - 1940 through until 1950.
Update 2017.

A Bletchley Alphabet.
Composed By Staff Members of Bletchley Park at the end of WWII.
Kindly Supplied by Mrs. Sharp.

A. Is for Anthony, our nominal head
    At least until the country went red
    We're Bevis Boys now and through Ernie's capers
    Poor Eden has had his redundancy papers.

B. Is for Budd, the Head of Hut Two
    Who hands out the wallop to me and to you
    When the Park closes down the last man to go
    Will be Mr. Budd, at least we hope so.
    (He was as we left in 1950, Dad closed the Park down, was Manager in 'C' Block)

C. Is for Crawley, our own dietician,
    Who serves up our grub like a mathematician
    It's round stodge or square, for the rest of your life
    Then eat the darn stuff without even a knife.

D. Is for Denny, his nickname is Stoker
    (We think, cos he peps up his pipe with a poker)
    He issues the Bronco and beer in a cask
    If it's not in the window, come in and ask.

E. Is for Sir Edward, the Gov'nor upstairs
    Who pinches our Clubroom for Christmas affair's
    He passes our transport, times without number
    In a pre-war upholstered beige coloured Humber.

F. Is for Foss – six foot in his shoes

Bletchley Park Family - 1940 through until 1950.
Update 2017.

    Seen in a kilt, but nir tartan troos
    If on a Friday a stroll you will take
    You'll find him dancing a reel by the lake.

G. Is for Griffith who finds us our digs
    Some live like princes, some live like pigs
    It's no good protesting, it's wasting your breath
    If you find your own Billet, he's tickled to death.

H. Is for Howgate, deceiver of WRENS
    He lures the poor creatures to dimly lit dens
    He twirls his moustache, is manly and curt
    But spoils the effect with an A.T.S. shirt.

I. Is for Intelligence, the Corps is in the Park
    They all need a haircut, but please keep it dark
    The question I hope to get answered one day
    Is how can a corpse be intelligent, pray.

J. Is for Joan, the Sec, of the Club
    Who chases you up for an overdue sub
    She lends you the Gatehouse – looks up your trains
    And then gets her flowers pinched for taking such pains.

K. Is for Kevin with hair slightly red
    A crescent shaped scar on the side of his head
    You may think he got it from some ancient dirk
    But he says his mother was hit by a Turk.

L. Is for Lowe, a clanking occurs
    Handlebar Harry is out with his spurs
    He doesn't claim to be much of a dancer

Bletchley Park Family - 1940 through until 1950.
Update 2017.

But what could you hope for from a Bengal Lancer.

M. Is for John Moore who's fungus ,tis said
   Allows him to carry on drinking in bed
   A slight overstatement his friends will retort
   For when fully loaded, it holds but a quart.

N. Is for Nenk, the Major in F
   When staff wanted leave he use to be deaf
   Now that his number is not far away
   He took them all out for a picnic one day.

O. Is for Owen, that's Dudley I mean
   When the curtain's gone up, he's not to be seen
   But if it come down in quite the wrong place
   It's Dudley, the stage boss, who loses his face.

P. Is for Parker, our check-suited dope
   Who thinks that his acting surpasses Bob Hope
   We know his forte's a bullocks front pins
   Who heard of a fan mail to 'Father of Twins'.

Q. Is for Tea, it's only a penny
   If there is cake it stretches to Fenny
   When work is a bore, and I'm sure you will see
   Lots on the TQ on the QT.

R. Is for Reiss, who can always be found
   With a large coloured brolly and two feet of hond
   When he goes up to Heaven and his name they record
   we hope they will ask "Is it down on the board".
S. Is for Sedgwick who ran all the hops

Bletchley Park Family - 1940 through until 1950.
Update 2017.

In the tough old days of American cops
Hush – Hush Whisper who dare
He slightly resembles that chap Fred Astaire.

T. Is for Tiltman just one of the boys
Red tabs he won't wear with brown corduroys
When Billets were scarce, Dame Rumour doth say
He lived in the States and flew in each day.

U. Is for Uncle Sam, who sent us some chaps
Three thousand miles to Bletchley perhaps
They came for the fashionable season
We are glad to have them, whatever the reason.

V. Is for Visitor, distinguished Brass-Hat
Comes snooping around to see what we're at
We sweep the place clean with dustpan and broom
And move all the empties to some other room.

W. Is for Wallace, the Colonel, you know
His name's at the end of a B.P.G.O.
He sits in a room that looks out on the grass
And forbids you to prop up your bike on the glass.

XYZ. Are frightful stinkers
We haven't one among our thinkers - hic - drinkers
And so perforce this daft effusion
We must bring now to a conclusion.
To the Inmates of B.P. from the Inmates of B.P. in grateful remembrance to the years we worked together.
1939 – 1945.

Bletchley Park Family - 1940 through until 1950.
Update 2017.

The Park itself had extensive woods and beautifully kept lawns which surrounded a decent size lake which at one time had about six small rowing boats on it, but when the war began for some unknown reason the boats were removed, maybe some government official in London thought a Submarine might surface and row German spies ashore; who would then be able to penetrate one of the most secret establishments of the Second World War, then they would see just how all the people working there managed to decipher the majority of German codes, my father never did understand the logic for this action, because when the boats were on the lake you could row out to the small island where the ducks would nest and if you didn't get caught you found nice fresh eggs.

The lake had lawns which at one time had been used for playing croquet, there were rose bushes and large hedges surrounding it, then at the top of one of the lawns near the Mansion were two of the most beautiful Magnolia trees a person could hope to see, and between them was situated a rose arch with steps leading down to the lawn.

Of course there were times when I would have to play with my two older sisters as we were the only children living in the park during the war, except for our older brother Bobbie who was 13 years older than I, so really he did not count as someone to play with, we were not allowed to have our friends come home with us; this was due to the very secret work, which was being carried out there, so, my sisters would be told they would have to look after me, which they of course did with all of the enthusiasm of them being placed into a room containing a swarm of bees.

Bletchley Park Family - 1940 through until 1950.
Update 2017.

Of course my sisters used to enjoy my presence, they would either try to, lose me, and then they would tell our mother I had run off, or make my life a total misery so eventually I would really run off, the outcome was inevitable anyway, when I arrived home I would get a clip around the ears, I had great sisters. The only way I can describe our Mother was I always thought our mum was the reincarnation of Hilda Baker remember her? She was the lady who always got her words wrong, things like, 'Sir Frances Drake circumcised the world with a big clipper' or when we lived in America she would say about the condominiums 'Oh look at those big Condoms' anyway, my sisters would have to suffer me for a few years yet, so when we did stay together, we would all go to the little hidden garden at the far end of the lake, the hedges were so high nobody could see what we were doing, it was our secret place, where we would tell our stories of pixies and fairies, dragons and kings, then we would have make believe tea parties and of course only the most important of people were invited.

One year my sisters decided to put on a pantomime for Christmas, it was called 'Pandora's Box' it was at this time I just happened to be suffering from 'Yellow Jaundice' so my two dear sisters decided that I would be a Chinaman in there play, I was all dressed out in a black pyjama suit mum had made with a small hat attached to which was a long black pigtail, how I hear you ask did a Chinaman happen to be in a Greek play put on as a Pantomime, that is one question I have tried to fathom out all my life, mind you I did make a very good Chinaman!!!!! During this pantomime Faye was to throw out all the bad demons etc. this being in the form of Tinsel and Paper represent the Demons; but my sister being enthusiastic about getting on stage (which NEVER happened) and her roll came

Bletchley Park Family - 1940 through until 1950.
Update 2017.

on at the wrong time and had to stay in the box, maybe that is why none of us ever thought of taking up acting as a career..

Life was great for a very young boy and his sisters who really didn't know what was happening on the front step let alone in the whole of the world, we never knew or understood what it was like to be on 'Rationing', Mum and Dad always made sure we had enough to eat I just do not know how they did it, I do remember dad always had a lot of chickens so we were never short of eggs or fresh chicken some weekends and of course Christmas, he also made sure the garden was dug over and planted with vegetables and in one place there was a strawberry plot, during the war I believe this was where the air raid shelter was and it was only after the war it was made into a strawberry bed, but I suppose all Mothers and Fathers were the same during this period of time.

At one time my sisters were given a couple of bicycles for their birthday, they were twins, their birthday was in April, and in fact it was the same date as Hitler's birthday, so they used to get teased real bad at school, anyway they had the bikes for presents, where dad got them from I will never know, they were the type we used to call 'sit up and beg', you know like the old 'sky pilot' (priest) used to ride, well of course when they got the bikes they were there pride and joy, and my not having a bike, they were told they had to let me have a go now and again, the answer, 'Nev can't ride a bike' and the retort from dad 'well teach him', (Bless you for this Dad) thanks dad, really Dad you did not know what you were letting your youngest son in for, because this now left me at the mercy of my two beloved sisters, there seemed to be a sadistic glow appear in their eyes, and you can just imagine the rubbing together of two pairs of

Bletchley Park Family - 1940 through until 1950.
Update 2017.

little hand, "Got you Nev" and they did, have you ever read the "Just William' stories, well just double him and his antics and you will know how much I suffered.

"Please hold the saddle; so I do not go too fast"

"Don't worry Nev we will look after you"

Yeah I know we have all heard that little phrase before

It's like Hitler saying he would not attack Poland or Russia, a lot of people believed him and I fell into the same trap with Jean and Faye.

We started off quite OK with Jean and Faye telling me they had a hold on the saddle, then their voices slowly faded into the distance as I went faster down the road between the Mansion and the Bungalow, the road outside the Mansion seemed to grow larger and nearer every second, the lake was getting larger and larger as I got closer to it, I could hear the twins voices so far behind me giggling like mad it is a wonder they were not rolling about on the road.

The ideal place to teach me to ride a bicycle was on the road between the Mansion and the bungalow, (the bungalow where Colossus the first ever electronic computer was 'Brain Stormed by Alan Turing, Max Newman and Tommy Flowers who are now credited as the Fathers of the modern computer, also based on Alan Turing's ideas the world of computing and the Internet originated) from the archway down to the roadway which was a nice little hill which led to the front of the Mansion, I was glad the lake wasn't at the bottom of this hill, (I could swear at times

Bletchley Park Family - 1940 through until 1950.
Update 2017.

I could see a gleam in my sisters eyes, as if they were willing the lake to move) I could just imagine the reply if I had gone in to the water, 'well you told us we had to teach him, can we help it if he can't steer properly'

I missed the main road and managed to fall off somewhere between the large lawn and the Mansion, never made it to the lake as I think dear twins were trying to get the bike to steer to it.

Jane Jenkins and David eventually moved into Number 3 Cottage, (where Alan Turing worked along with Alfred Dillwyn Knox for a while, Turing use to have his tea and sugar delivered and hoisted them up to one of the upstairs windows which was over the back door at the side of Number 3 Cottage and NOT as it has been said, through the windows of the Tower in Number 2 Cottage, as really THIS would have been a feat worthy of an Illusionist as THIS was NOT a room but our stairway upstairs and me being a VERY adventurous young boy I would NEVER have tried to reach the windows), the friendship of Jane and David was appreciated very much as we spent most of the time together playing all over the Park.

Jane!!! I think she was just a bit older than I was but the three of us spent a lot of time together and looking back on those times I remember Jane as being a real 'Tomboy' if we climbed the tallest tree's she wasn't far behind us, playing cowboys and Indians she was always there to join in the fun, getting tied up against a pole and us acting like Indians, she was always willing to go and do anything David and I were also willing to do for a dare, poor Jane usually landed up as the "Baddy", I met Jane again for a very short get together, when the Duke of Kent

Bletchley Park Family - 1940 through until 1950.
Update 2017.

opened the Park as a Museum for Code Breaking, and looking back wish very much we could have spent some time together reminiscing over old times at Bletchley Park, I am sure we would have had a very good laugh at the antics we all got up to.

Of course it was not always fun and games, there were times when we were told we couldn't go to certain areas of the park to play, well, you must realise it is like showing a red flag to a bull, especially to my sisters, Neville always got caught and dragged home by one of the special security guards to face mum and dad, and yes, I always got the clip around the ear, while dear sisters stood by like two little angels as if butter wouldn't melt in their mouths.

The house we lived in at the Park was Number 2 Cottage, this was set to the side of the Mansion behind large trees and hedges, it had a court yard which had two other houses one either side of Number 2 Cottage; at the top end of the yard were the old stables and coach sheds, then leading out of the yard you had to pass under an old clock arch from which when you looked down the road was the back gate, this road was lined by the garden outhouses and garages.

As you entered the cottage, in front of you was a long hallway with six rooms leading off from it, first on the left was my Sisters Jean and Faye's bedroom, next was our Brother Bobby's bedroom then the last door on the left was the large living room, this had two big windows looking out over our garden, I remember this room being decorated at some time by some of the men who worked for the M.O.W. during the war you could not get wallpaper so the whole room was painted by hand, I hear what you say, so what, well I do not mean the paint was

Bletchley Park Family - 1940 through until 1950.
Update 2017.

just slapped onto the walls; all of the patterns were hand painted, the lines for each panel and then the dapple pattern in the panels were completed with sponges; mind you they only had a few colours to choose from, green, white, black or brown, that last one, I'm really not sure of.

At the end of the hall facing the front door was the bathroom then next to this was a very large kitchen; it really was the main room of the house, in one corner was the largest larder you ever saw, I should know, if they lost me, it was the first place they would look, I could get a chair inside, shut the door and have a good old feast, mum was a very good cook and could make our food go quite a long way, also dad kept chickens so we were never without fresh eggs or for that matter chickens, I can sometimes still smell the food dad use to mix for the chickens, potato and carrot skins, all of the greens tops had been cut away and any other scraps, which were left over, these were all mixed together and then cooked on the stove and mixed with corn, we also had to save all of the eggshells then we would crush and grill them this was put out for the chickens to eat; boy did they produce some good eggs, dad also kept a vegetable garden, so the larder was the place to be, I mean it would be pure madness to run away from home and leave all of this, so I would shut myself away with beautiful home made jams, pickles and pies all stored on an old marble slab, to this day I still enjoy all of the home made treats but most of all I remember those early days sitting in the larder, great.

A radio was situated next to the old black leaded stove, which was still in use although our mother did have a gas cooker, mum and dad listening to the news in the evenings and later have the most popular show of the times I.T.M.A. as many of

Bletchley Park Family - 1940 through until 1950.
Update 2017.

the older generation will know stands for 'It's That Man Again' then after ward the News and then I was always ready for 'Dick Barton, Special Agent' supported as always by his good friends Jock and Snowy, as soon as this programme was finished it was off to bed.

There were a few other radio shows for the kids during this period, such as 'Journey Into Space' another "Archie Andrews' now you have to understand this period during and just after WWII, if I tell you Archie Andrews was a ventriloquist dummy, the ventriloquist name was Peter Brough, now I hear you ask how could people listen to a radio show featuring a wooden dummy, as I said there were a few radio shows and not many televisions about in fact very few, dad did manage to get hold of a TV very soon after the war, how I will never know, the screen was about 9" across so we had a magnifying screen over it so we could all see it together, TV programmes were only on for about 1 hour at midday which was usually a film for demonstration purposes, 1 hour in the afternoon with programmes like 'Jam Session' which was swing music followed by the 'News Reel' and then 'Picture Page' a topical magazine 175th Edition and 2¾ hours in the evening this usually started about 8:00pm until about 10:50pm and was sometimes in sound only, (I hear what you're saying: they have a Ventriloquist dummy on radio who you can't see and then in the evening they have a sound only programme on television, whoever worked out these programmes must have had a great sense of humour), this was followed at 9:00pm by something called 'Cabaret' 9:30pm 'News Reel' usually the same as the morning show 9:30am 'News Reel', 9:40pm 'Picture Page' once more the same as the morning and eventually closing with the 'News' at 10:25 until 10:45pm and close down with the

Bletchley Park Family - 1940 through until 1950.
Update 2017.

National Anthem, so there was nothing to watch all through the day and well into the night as we have these days.

The last room on the ground floor was mum and dads, this was just inside to the right of the front door, I think they had this room as dad sometimes had to go out in the middle of the night, we used to get calls at all hours of the day or night, and you had to go through this room to get to the stairway, where there was a doorway leading to a spiral stair onto a landing where all of our toys were stored, this landing then opened on a large 'L' shaped room with two smaller rooms at the back of the house, one of these being mine, after the war as Anne and Madge, the two ATS drivers lived with us. no, I did not mind being upstairs by myself, in fact I enjoyed it, it was like my place where I could get away from everything and everybody, where I could play as I wanted without interruption from my sisters or brother.

at nights sometimes I would lay in bed and listen to the drone of the aircraft flying overhead, wondering where they were going and what the outcome would be when they reached their targets, the sound seemed to go on and on all night long, I never knew if they were German aircraft or our own, but, it is a sound that I will never forget, also I really do not think I will ever hear it again, also the TRUMPING sound of the DOODLEBUGS as they went over and then the noise just stops that was the scary time, although at times they have tried to recreate it in the movies but never seem to get it right, sometimes on a warm summers night when there is no other sound to disturb the air, you may hear a plane fly overhead and it does jog something from the back of your mind, it takes you back to those times when to you, not much seemed to matter except you could do

Bletchley Park Family - 1940 through until 1950.
Update 2017.

what you wanted, it's such an individual sound, a deep drone that seemed to go up and down in pitch, also some nights we would sit on the bench seats in the windows and see the searchlights to the south of us, they would criss cross the sky with an eerie sense of probing, it was like a light show which went on for hours, during the days we would watch the vapour trails from the planes overhead, they use to leave such lovely patterns in the sky, but then only being children how were we to know what really was going on up there, well, my brother and sisters did but with me it was so different, it was only when I was a bit older I began to realise what was happening.

When we went to school in St Mary's School Church Green Road, we would go out by the Back Gate, across Rickley Lane and through a spinney to the gate, which lead to St Mary's churchyard, through the gate and down the drive, pass the memorial of the First World War, then on down Church Green Road past another building which we were told was a Private School but since then we have learned it was where more people from Bletchley Park worked, then on to the recreation park by the school for a quick swing or a ride on the roundabout before classes began.

Then all too soon the school bell would ring and we would have to go into the old classrooms with the high ceilings, with those old dusty wooden beams and in the middle of the room were the "Pot Bellied" fires, which were supposed to keep the whole room warm but we would still try and get the desks, you remember those desks they were all in one with the inkwell in, nearest to the fire, and all the older children seem to vie to be the 'Ink Monitor', a job which I shunned away from, as it was in

Bletchley Park Family - 1940 through until 1950.
Update 2017.

my opinion the dirtiest thing to do, if it was the cleanest the teacher wouldn't let the kids do it.

I always seemed to get very dirty at school (even though I steered clear of being the 'Ink Monitor') with all of those games during playtime and of course mum would ask for my clothes so she could wash them and she would then have to go through the pockets to empty them, this she always did with care as she would never know what she might find, she really did not know what wonders she was about to find, things all small boys cherish. The odd piece of string, it had so many uses, it was the spare conker string, or to tie up your shoe when the lace was broken, and a broken lace always seemed to happen because of the games we used to play, it was a make believe lasso, it was so many different things in a child's mind.

There was the cap bomb; this was a tear drop shaped piece of lead which looked like an aircraft, cut in half at the middle to give you a top and a bottom so the caps could be placed inside, and it was held together with, what else, but with the ever useful piece of string, and then when you threw it into the air and it went as high as you could see, it would drop down to earth and land with such a noise, the caps would explode just like a real bomb, or so you thought.

Then there was the Almond nut whistle; the Almond was rubbed against a wall as you walked home from school, by doing this you would make one end flat until a small hole appeared, then you would make another hole on the side near the hole at the end, this was also achieved by rubbing the nut against the top corner of the brick wall, and what you ended up with was a nice little whistle.

Bletchley Park Family - 1940 through until 1950.
Update 2017.

What was the other things mum would find in my pockets? Well now let me see, there was the penknife, spare wheels for my Dinky Toy's, half eaten toffee's, exploding caps for my bomb, a Dinky Toy racing car, the fastest in the school I might add, a very small stub of a pencil, some screwed up paper, for that very important note you may have to pass to a classmate, or a girlfriend! The males in our family always grew up very fast, and a few other items, which always seemed to come in handy, or at least I thought they would, but mum always had different Ideas.

After school had finished and we had managed to get back into the park, we had our tea and then we would sometimes go with mum and dad to the club house they used to run; after the war, which was situated next to the Mansion, it was in a long old hut which use to be the Navy Intelligence Hut 4, which had a couple of billiard tables in the room on the left as you went in, a long lounge to the right with the bar at the far end, beyond this was a dance room, which is where I would spend a lot of my time playing records of all of the best bands of the time, Glen Miller, Benny Goodman, Ted Heath (no not the ex-prime minister) and so many more, Al Bowlly singing with Ronnie Munro, Reginald Williams, and Ken 'Snakehips' Johnson bands, in fact I still have and love some of these records and play them, they bring back so many memories and in some way seem to have a soothing action and bring back some lovely recollections, in the evenings sometime there would be dances and of course I would be invited to put the records on.

Other times I would sit just inside the servery and one of the ladies, her name was Moira, (the good things just seem to stick

Bletchley Park Family - 1940 through until 1950.
Update 2017.

in your memory, because she was a very beautiful woman) who was stationed in the park, she would always come straight to talk to me, I think this was my first love I was about Eight years old at the time, we mature early in our family, but as usual I took a lot of stick from my brother and sisters over it.

My brother Bobbie told us once about two men who worked on the code breaking called Nick and Willie one day they came into the club house and bought a couple of pints of beer, then they raised their glasses and said "Here's to 66-44", we never did understand what the importance was of what they were saying at the time, at least not until after the war, when it was explained as the date of the invasion into Europe "6th of June 1944.

We always seemed to have great snowy winters; the snow was so deep it nearly came over the top of our Wellington's, and then we would build the big snow castles on the lawn opposite the Mansion and waylay the people who worked in the park with snowballs as they went to have lunch and then on their return from the canteen.

I think this was such a diversion from the work they did all day, listening to the radios and trying to fathom out which codes were in use at the time, sometimes we would get chased all over the park with people trying to hit us with snowballs.

Some of the Christmas presents we used to get, were nothing really fancy just a few things which mum and dad managed to put together, a couple I remember, one was a boat in the shape

Bletchley Park Family - 1940 through until 1950.
Update 2017.

of a freighter (the plan of which was issued in the Daily Mirror) which was made by some of the men who worked opposite the

Bletchley Park Family - 1940 through until 1950.
Update 2017.

motor pool workshops, I think they were to do with the maintenance department for the Ministry of Works, the man in charge, if I remember was called Mr Bob Watson Senior, this boat was one of the best presents I think I have ever received, the bow and the stern were made of solid wood, and the two sides, decks and the bottom were pieces of plywood, the superstructure was made of assorted pieces of wood, and the bridge was in two layers with the funnels fitting in between some of these pieces, and underneath in what I suppose you would call the hold was a cut down mouse trap, when loaded and the spring held in place by a round peg of wood which protruded through the side of the boat about a quarter of an inch from the bottom, this was just the right height so when a large marble was rolled at it and if you were good enough to hit this peg, then the decks and the superstructure would be thrown up into the air just like a real exploding ship, just the right sort of toy for a young boy to have during wartime, Jean and Faye had some wooden sewing boxes made with marquetry overlay.

Toward the end of the War and just after there would be some entertainment shows put on at the Assembly Hall by the residence of the Park.

Dad setting up the trestle tables in the entrance hall for the drinks and mum putting out sandwiches and other food.

Both my sisters and I remember some of the acts, there was impersonations of Abbot and Costello doing their act about Baseball:-

I have managed to find the whole script which now I have read it seems rather mundane but was funny at the time.

Bletchley Park Family - 1940 through until 1950.
Update 2017.

(Lou Costello is considering becoming a ballplayer. Bud Abbott wants to make sure he knows what he's getting into.)

Abbott: Strange as it may seem, they give ball players nowadays very peculiar names.

Costello: Funny names?

Abbott: Nicknames, nicknames. Now, on the St. Louis team we have Who's on first, What's on second, I Don't Know is on third--

Costello: That's what I want to find out. I want you to tell me the names of the fellows on the St. Louis team.

Abbott: I'm telling you. Who's on first, What's on second, I Don't Know is on third--

Costello: You know the fellows' names?

Abbott: Yes.

Bletchley Park Family - 1940 through until 1950.
Update 2017.

Costello: Well, then who's playing first?

Abbott: Yes.

Costello: I mean the fellow's name on first base.

Abbott: Who.

Costello: The fellow playin' first base.

Abbott: Who.

Costello: The guy on first base.

Abbott: Who is on first.

Costello: Well, what are you askin' me for?

Abbott: I'm not asking you--I'm telling you. Who is on first.

Costello: I'm asking you--who's on first?

Abbott: That's the man's name.

Costello: That's who's name?

Abbott: Yes.

Costello: When you pay off the first baseman every month, who gets the money?

Abbott: Every dollar of it. And why not, the man's entitled to it.

Bletchley Park Family - 1940 through until 1950.
Update 2017.

Costello: Who is?

Abbott: Yes.

Costello: So who gets it?

Abbott: Why shouldn't he? Sometimes his wife comes down and collects it.

Costello: Who's wife?

Abbott: Yes. After all, the man earns it.

Costello: Who does?

Abbott: Absolutely.

Costello: Well, all I'm trying to find out is what's the guy's name on first base?

Abbott: Oh, no, no. What is on second base?

Costello: I'm not asking you who's on second.

Abbott: Who's on first!

Costello: St. Louis has a good outfield?

Abbott: Oh, absolutely.

Costello: The left fielder's name?

Bletchley Park Family - 1940 through until 1950.
Update 2017.

Abbott: Why.

Costello: I don't know, I just thought I'd ask.

Abbott: Well, I just thought I'd tell you.

Costello: Then tell me who's playing left field?

Abbott: Who's playing first.

Costello: Stay out of the infield! The left fielder's name?

Abbott: Why.

Costello: Because.

Abbott: Oh, he's centre field.

Costello: Wait a minute. You got a pitcher on this team?

Abbott: Wouldn't this be a fine team without a pitcher?

Costello: Tell me the pitcher's name.

Abbott: Tomorrow.

Costello: Now, when the guy at bat bunts the ball--me being a good catcher--I want to throw the guy out at first base, so I pick up the ball and throw it to who?

Abbott: Now, that's the first thing you've said right.

Bletchley Park Family - 1940 through until 1950.
Update 2017.

Costello: I DON'T EVEN KNOW WHAT I'M TALKING ABOUT!

Abbott: Don't get excited. Take it easy.

Costello: I throw the ball to first base, whoever it is grabs the ball, so the guy runs to second. Who picks up the ball and throws it to what. What throws it to I don't know. I don't know throws it back to tomorrow--a triple play.

Abbott: Yeah, it could be.

Costello: Another guy gets up and it's a long ball to centre.

Abbott: Because.

Costello: Why? I don't know. And I don't care.

Abbott: What was that?

Costello: I said, I DON'T CARE!

Abbott: Oh, that's our shortstop!

Bletchley Park Family - 1940 through until 1950.
Update 2017.

Then there were three young ladies who took off the 'Andrew Sisters'

Two men who impersonated 'Flannigan and Allen' singing 'Underneath the Arches' usually Flannigan dress in a long Muskrat coat (a medium-sized semi-aquatic rodent native to North America) and wearing a straw boater hat with the front of the rim turned up, Allen usually dressed in a smart suite and a 'Spiv' type fedora hat.

Bletchley Park Family - 1940 through until 1950.
Update 2017.

Underneath the arches,
We dream our dreams away,
Underneath the arches,
On cobblestones we lay.
Back to back we're sleeping,
Tired out and Worn,
Happy when the daylight comes creeping,
Heralding the dawn.

Sleeping when it's raining,
And sleeping when it's fine,
Trains rattling by above.
Pavement is my pillow,
No matter where I roam,
Underneath the arches,
We dream our dreams of home.

One of the places everyone met was at 'Greens Café' (Bit of a dive really but it was the only Café with music blaring out all the time) which was situated on the Main Bletchley Road, now 'Queensway' just along from the 'Park Hotel', then there was the 'Odeon Cinema' on the Main Road where Bobby use to take me to watch the latest Cowboy films, Saturday Morning Pictures were shown at the 'County' sixpence downstairs and a shilling for the balcony.

The films shown on a Saturday were Roy Rodgers and his wonder Horse Trigger, Flash Gordon, Tom Mix, Hopalong Cassidy, Dick Tracy, Bug's Bunny, and Superman with a couple more very amateur Space stories.

Bletchley Park Family - 1940 through until 1950.
Update 2017.

We lived at Bletchley Park until 1950, Jean has enjoyed being a voluntary Steward at Bletchley Park for the last 20 years; we all loved the place and have so many happy childhood memories.

The conversations with some of the visitors can be very interesting. On duty one Sunday, a lady named Pauline found out who Jean was and said "I can remember a smiling head of dispatch" she was referring to our father another lady named Elizabeth was very pleased to speak to Jean about our family. She wrote Jean a letter saying "It was a pleasure to meet you Jean and talk about my dear old friends the Budd's; like so many I was only 18/19 when I joined Bletchley Park and your mum and dad kept a watchful eye on us and became our 2nd parents." It gave Jean a great thrill to find out things like that about our parents.

Other people Jean has met when on duty are old school friends and a girl, Marcia who was a bridesmaid at Jeans wedding. The biggest thrill Jean had was when a young lady asked her where number 2 cottage was, as her Grandma used to live there during the war; she turned out to be our long lost niece from our brother Bobs first marriage.

As a family we are now a bit widespread. Unfortunately our brother Bob died 8th April 2000 and Neville lived in South Africa until 2013 when he returned to England after the death of his wife Sally, our sister Faye living in Australia with her family; She is the one who made the wall hanging in the hallway of the mansion.

Jean still lives in the UK where she LOVES go to the park as a steward and often come in to volunteer twice a month to do

Bletchley Park Family - 1940 through until 1950.
Update 2017.

duty in the Bletchley Park Post Office. and enjoys the times spent reminiscing about the Park with Visitors.

The thing I remember best was the VE service, which was held on the lawn in front of the Mansion with all of the flags flying, people dancing and singing it was just like people were making up for all of the parties that had been denied them throughout the war, and with the end of the war at last they really let their hair down.

When the war had ended we were allowed to have some friends visit us in the Park, some such occasions were birthday parties, I remember one, maybe it was the first one after the war, when my sisters Jean and Faye invited some of the girls from their class at Bletchley Road School, they were all gathered on the big lawn at the lake near the two beautiful Magnolia trees, it was only at this time that a lot of our friends realised the size and beauty of our garden.

In a way I am grateful I lived through this period of time, the events which happened, the beautiful music of the period, i.e. Glen Miller, the Dorsey Brothers, Frank Sinatra, The Andrews Sisters and so many more, the people I met, who did so much for our country but remained quiet about their achievements, the trust and camaraderie, also to know in some way that the family I was part of played such an important role in the history of this world.

ABOUT THE AUTHOR

Bletchley Park Family - 1940 through until 1950.
Update 2017.

I was born in Portsmouth, Royal Naval & Marine Maternity Hospital 1st October 1938.

We moved to Hayes, Middlesex in 1940 and then to Bletchley Park, where my father worked during WWII in 1940 through until 1950 with my twin sisters and older brother, we moved to the Plough Inn at Simpson, Near Bletchley.

In 1950, I attended the Royal Hospital School; Holbrook, which before it moved there in 1932 it was the Royal Palace at Greenwich, donated by the then King William and Queen Mary to be converted into an Institution for Relief and Support of Seamen.

I left in 1955 and joined the Royal Navy until 1960, as a Voice Radio & RADAR Operator Served on various ships and shore stations in England, Mediterranean and the Far East as RADAR Operator & Plotter, communications ship/aircraft and on Coast Watching Duties in the Far East.

After leaving the Royal Navy I worked in various countries as an Industrial Radiologist and then as a Professional Engineer in Industrial Efficiency and Quality Assurance/Quality Control for 53 years.

In 1959 on July the 25th, I married Sarah Doreen Charnock and lived in Leighton Buzzard until 1983.

I retired 3 years ago and needed something to occupy myself with as due to my wife being virtually house bound I really

Bletchley Park Family - 1940 through until 1950.
Update 2017.

could not leave her by herself and became a House Husband and during my spare time------writing.

My beautiful wife died 27th Nov 2012, so I returned to England

I know this is a bit long but I have been around for a LONG time 78 years.

Neville J. Budd.

'When someone shares with you something of value, you have an obligation to share it with others'

Chinese Proverb

Printed in Great Britain
by Amazon